Differentiating Instruction With Menus

for the *Inclusive Classroom*

Language Arts

LOWER & ON-LEVEL MENUS
GRADES 3–5

Differentiating Instruction With Menus

for the Inclusive Classroom

Language Arts

Laurie E. Westphal

PRUFROCK PRESS INC.
WACO, TEXAS

Library of Congress Cataloging-in-Publication Data

Westphal, Laurie E., 1967-
  Differentiating instruction with menus for the inclusive classroom. Language arts, grades 3-5 / by Laurie E. Westphal.
    p. cm.
  Includes bibliographical references.
  ISBN 978-1-59363-885-6 (pbk.)
  1. Language arts (Elementary) 2. Individualized instruction. 3. Inclusive education. 4. Mixed ability grouping in education. I. Title.

  LB1576.W4846 2012
  372.6--dc23

             2011050398

Edited by Sarah Morrison
Production Design by Raquel Trevino

ISBN-13: 978-1-59363-885-6

Printed in the United States of America.

At the time of this book's publication, all facts and figures cited are the most current available; all telephone numbers, addresses, and website URLs are accurate and active; all publications, organizations, websites, and other resources exist as described in this book; and all have been verified. The author and Prufrock Press make no warranty or guarantee concerning the information and materials given out by organizations or content found at websites, and we are not responsible for any changes that occur after this book's publication. If you find an error or believe that a resource listed here is not as described, please contact Prufrock Press.

Prufrock Press Inc.
P.O. Box 8813
Waco, TX 76714-8813
Phone: (800) 998-2208
Fax: (800) 240-0333
http://www.prufrock.com

CONTENTS

Author's Note

If you are familiar with books on various differentiation strategies, you probably know about the Differentiating Instruction With Menus series. You may be flipping through this book and wondering how this series differs from that series, as well as whether you need to purchase a book from that series in order to use a book from this one. In fact, when we first discussed adding this series to the menu product line, my editor wondered how this new series could be designed so that the two series wouldn't "cannibalize" (graphic, but a great word!) one another. Here is the essential relationship between the two series as I see it: **These two menus series stand on their own if you have students of fairly similar ability levels. This series, Differentiating Instruction With Menus for the Inclusive Classroom, provides menus for the lower level, on-level, and ELL students, whereas the original series provides menus for the on-level, advanced, and gifted students. If you work with a wide range of student abilities (from special needs to gifted), these two series can be used as companions. When used together, they provide a total of three tiered menu options for each topic of study.** The menus in this book are made to complement the menus in the original series, and they are coded so that they are easily distinguishable from one another. Each set of menus in this book is made up of a lower level menu, designated by a small triangle symbol in the upper right-hand corner, and a middle-level menu, designated by a small circle symbol in the upper right-hand corner. The menus contained in the corresponding volume of the original series (*Differentiating Instruction With Menus: Language Arts* for grades 3–5) can be used as options for more advanced students.

Many teachers have told me how helpful the Differentiating Instruction With Menus books are and how they have modified the books to meet the needs of their students—by purchasing the K–2 books in addition to the 3–5 books for their fourth-grade classes, for instance, or by using menus from the 3–5 books in some of their ninth-grade classrooms. Teachers are always the first to tweak things to make them work, but I thought it would be great if those teachers had a tool that did all of that work for them. Thus, the Differentiating Instruction With Menus for the Inclusive Classroom series was born.

The menu designs used in this book (and the rest of the books in this series) reflect a successful modification technique that I started using in my classroom as the range of my students' ability levels widened. I experimented with many ways to use menus, from having all students use the same menu with the same expectations, to having everyone use the same menu with modified contracted expectations, to giving each student one of three leveled menus with some overlapping activities based on readiness, ability, and/or preassessment results. I found that if the ability levels among my students during a certain school year were closer, I could use one menu for everyone with only slight modifications; however, the greater the span of my students' abilities became, the more I needed a variety of leveled menus to reach everyone. Each book in the Differentiating Instruction With Menus for the Inclusive Classroom series, with its two leveled menus for the objectives covered, can fill this need, providing more options for students with diverse abilities in the inclusive classroom.

—Laurie E. Westphal

CHAPTER 1

Choice

Choice in the Inclusive Classroom

Let's begin by addressing the concept of the inclusive classroom. The term inclusive (vs. exclusive) leads one to believe that we are discussing a situation in which all students are included. In the simplest of terms, that is exactly what we are referring to as an inclusive classroom: a classroom that may have special needs students, on-level students, bilingual or ESL students, and gifted students. Although the concept is a simple one, the considerations are significant.

When thinking about the inclusive classroom and its unique ambiance, one must first consider the needs of the range of students within the classroom. Mercer and Lane (1996) stated it best in their assessment of the needs in an inclusive classroom:

> Students who are academically gifted, those who have had abundant experiences, and those who have demonstrated proficiency with lesson content typically tend to perform well when instruction is anchored at the "implicit" end of the instructional continuum. In contrast, low-performing students (i.e., students at risk for school failure, students with learning disabilities, and students with other special

needs) and students with limited experience or proficiency with lesson content are most successful when instruction is explicit. Students with average academic performance tend to benefit most from the use of a variety of instructional methods that address individual needs. Instructional decisions for most students, therefore, should be based on assessment of individual needs. (pp. 230–231)

Acknowledging these varied and often contradictory needs that arise within an inclusive classroom can lead to frustration when trying to make one assignment or task fit everyone's needs. There are few—if any—traditional, teacher-directed lessons that can be implicit, explicit, and based on individual needs all at the same time. There is, however, one *technique* that tries to accomplish this: choice.

Choice: The Superman of Techniques?

Can the offering of appropriate choices really be the hero of the inclusive classroom? Can it leap buildings in a single bound and meet the needs of our implicit, explicit, and individual interests? Yes. By considering the use and benefits of choice, we can see that by offering choices, teachers really can meet the needs of the whole range of students in an inclusive classroom. Ask adults whether they would prefer to choose what to do or be told what to do, and of course, they will say they would prefer to have a choice. Students have the same feelings. Although they may not be experienced in making choices, they will make choices based on their needs, just as adults—which makes everyone involved in the inclusive experience a little less stressed and frustrated.

One benefit of choice is its ability to meet the needs of so many different students and their learning styles. The Dunedin College of Education (Keen, 2001) conducted a research study on the preferred learning styles of 250 gifted students. Students were asked to rank different learning options. Of the 13 different options described to the students, only one option did not receive at least one negative response: the option of having choice. All students have different learning styles and preferences, yet choice is the one option that meets all students' needs. Students, be they gifted or special needs, are going to choose what best fits their own learning styles and educational needs.

> ## "I am different in the way I do stuff. I like to build stuff with my hands."
>
> *—Sixth-grade student, when asked why he enjoyed activities that allow choice*

Another benefit of choice is a greater sense of independence for the students, some who have not had the opportunity to think about their own learning in the past. What a powerful feeling! Students will be designing and creating products based on what they envision, rather than what their teacher envisions. There is a possibility for more than one "right" product; all students can make products their own, no matter their level of ability. When students would enter my classroom, they had often been trained by previous teachers to produce exactly what the teacher wanted, not what the students thought would be best. Teaching my students that what they envisioned could be correct (and wonderful) was often a struggle. "Is this what you want?" and "Is this right?" were popular questions as we started the school year. Allowing students to have choices in the products they create to demonstrate their learning helps create independence at any age, within any ability level.

Strengthened student focus on the required content is a third benefit. When students have choices in the activities they wish to complete, they are more focused on the learning that leads to their choice product. Students become excited when they learn information that can help them develop a product they would like to create. Students pay close attention to instruction and have an immediate application for the knowledge being presented in class. Also, if students are focused, they are less likely to be off task during instruction.

The final benefit (although I am sure there are many more) is the simple fact that by offering varied choices at appropriate levels, you can address implicit instructional options, explicit instructional options, and individual needs without anyone getting overly frustrated or overworked. Many a great educator has referred to the idea that the best learning takes place when the students have a desire to learn and can feel successful while doing it. Some students have a desire to be taught information, others prefer to explore and learn things that are new to them; still others do not want to learn anything unless it is of interest to them. By choosing from different activities according to their interests and readiness, students stretch beyond what they already know, and by offering such choices, teachers create a void that needs to be filled. This void leads to a desire to learn.

A Point to Ponder: Making Good Choices Is a Skill

> ## "I wanted you to know, I never thought of [good choices as a skill] that way. That really opened my eyes."
>
> *—Kindergarten teacher, after hearing me discuss choice as a skill*

When we think of making a good choice as a skill, much like writing an effective paragraph, it becomes easy enough to understand the processes needed to encourage students to make their own choices. In keeping with this analogy, students could certainly figure out how to write on their own, and perhaps even how to compose sentences and paragraphs, by modeling other examples. Imagine, however, the progress and strength of the writing produced when students are given guidance and even the most basic of instruction on how to accomplish the task. The written piece is still their own, but the quality of the finished piece is much stronger when guidance is given during the process. The same is true with the quality of choices students can make in the classroom.

As with writing, students—especially those with special needs—could make choices on their own, but when the teacher provides background knowledge and assistance, the choices become more meaningful and the products richer. Although all students certainly need guidance, the on-level and special needs students often will need the most guidance; they have usually not been in an educational setting that has allowed them to experience different products, and the idea of choice can be new to them. Some students may have experienced only basic instructional choices, like choosing between two journal prompts or perhaps having the option of making either a poster or a PowerPoint presentation about the content being studied. Some may not have experienced even this level of choice. This lack of experience can cause frustration for both teacher and student.

Teaching Choices as a Skill

So, what is the best way to provide guidance and enable students to develop the skill of making good choices? First, choose the appropriate number of choices for your students. Although the goal might be to have students choose from nine different options, teachers might start by having their students choose from three predetermined choices the first day (if they were using a shape menu, for instance, students might choose a circle activity). Then, after those products had been created, students could choose from another three options a few days later, and perhaps from another three the following week. By breaking students' choices down, teachers reinforce how to approach or attack a more complex and/or varied choice format in the future. All students can work up to making complex choices from longer lists of options as their choice skill level increases.

Second, students will need guidance on how to select the option that is right for them. They may not automatically gravitate towards options without an exciting and detailed description of each choice. For the most part, students have been trained to produce what the teacher requests, which means that when given a choice, they will usually choose what they think will please the teacher. This means that when the teacher discusses the different menu options, he or she has to be equally as excited about each option. The discussion of the different choices has to be animated and specific. For example, if the content is all very similar, the focus should be on the product: "If you want to do some singing, this one is for you!" or "If you want to write and draw, circle this one as a maybe!" Sometimes, options may differ based on both content and product, in which case both can be pointed out to students to assist them in making a good choice for themselves. "You have some different choices in our life cycle unit. If you want to do something with animals and drawing, check this one as a maybe. If you are thinking you want to do something with leaf collecting and making a speech, this one might be for you!" The more exposure students have to the processing the teacher provides, the more skillful they become in their choice making.

How Can Teachers Provide Choices?

> "I have seen my behavior issues significantly decrease when my students have choices. I wasn't expecting that at all—I thought that they would be off ask and harder to control."
>
> *—Fifth-grade inclusion teacher, when asked how his students with special needs respond to having choices*

When people go to a restaurant, the common goal is to find something on the menu to satisfy their hunger. Students come into our classrooms having a hunger, as well—a hunger for learning. Choice menus are a way of allowing our students to choose how they would like to satisfy that hunger. At the very least, a menu is a list of choices that students use to choose an activity (or activities) they would like to complete to show what they have learned. At best, it is a complex system in which students earn points by making choices from different areas of study. All menus should also incorporate a free-choice option for those "picky eaters" who would like to make a special order to satisfy their learning hunger.

The next few sections provide examples of the main types of menus that will be used in this book. Each menu has its own benefits, limitations or drawbacks, and time considerations. An explanation of the free-choice option and its management will follow the information on each type of menu.

Three Shape Menu

> "I like the flexibility of the Three Shape menu. I can give students just one strip of shapes or the entire menu depending on their readiness."
>
> *—Third-grade teacher*

Description

The Three Shape menu (see Figure 1.1) is a basic menu with a total of nine predetermined choices for students. The choices are created at

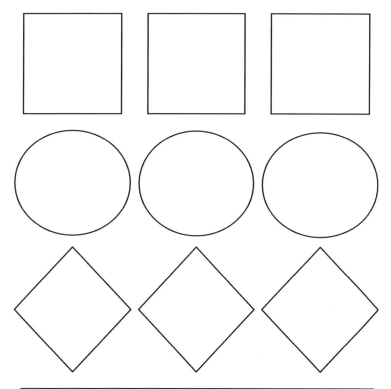

Figure 1.1. Three Shape menu.

the various levels of Bloom's Revised taxonomy (Anderson & Krathwohl, 2001) and incorporate different learning styles. All products carry the same weight for grading and have similar expectations for completion time and effort.

Benefits

Flexibility. This menu can cover one topic in depth, or three different objectives. When this menu covers just one objective, students have the option of completing three products: one from each shape group.

Friendly design. Students quickly understand how to use this menu. It is easy to explain how to make the choices based on the various shapes, and the shapes can be used to visually separate expectations (e.g., circles one week, squares the next).

Weighting. All products are equally weighted, so recording grades and maintaining paperwork is easily accomplished with this menu.

Short time period. They are intended for shorter periods of time, between 1–3 weeks.

Limitations

Few topics. These menus only cover one or three topics.

Time Considerations

These menus are usually intended for shorter amounts of completion time—at the most, they should take 3 weeks. If the menu focuses on one topic in depth, it could be completed in 1 week.

Tic-Tac-Toe Menu

> ## "Sometimes I only liked two, but I had to do three."
>
> —*Second-grade student, when asked what he liked least about a menu used in his classroom*

Description

The Tic-Tac-Toe menu (see Figure 1.2) is a well-known, commonly used menu that contains a total of eight predetermined choices and, if appropriate, one free choice for students. Choices can be created at the same level of Bloom's Revised taxonomy or can be arranged in such a way to allow for the three different levels or content areas. If all choices have been created at the same level of Bloom's Revised taxonomy, then each choice carries the same weight for grading and has similar expectations for completion time and effort.

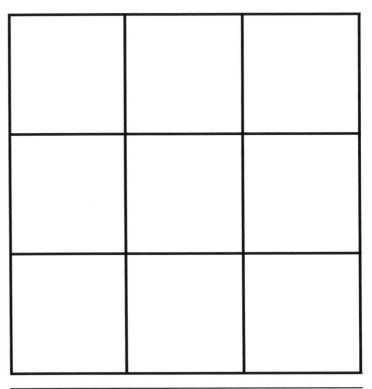

Figure 1.2. Tic-Tac-Toe menu.

Benefits

Flexibility. This menu can cover either one topic in depth or three different topics, objectives, or even content areas. When this menu covers just one objective and all tasks are from the same level of Bloom's Revised taxonomy, students have the option of completing three projects in a tic-tac-toe pattern, or simply picking three from the menu. When the menu covers three objectives or different levels of Bloom's Revised taxonomy, students will need to complete a tic-tac-toe pattern (either a vertical column or horizontal row) to be sure they have completed one activity from each objective or level.

Stretching. When students make choices on this menu, completing a row or column based on its design, they will usually face one choice that is out of their comfort zone, be it for its level of Bloom's Revised taxonomy, its product learning style, or its content. They will complete this "uncomfortable" choice because they want to do the other two in that row or column.

Friendly design. Students quickly understand how to use this menu. It is nonthreatening because it does not contain points, and therefore it seems to encourage students to stretch out of their comfort zones.

Weighting. All projects are equally weighted, so recording grades and maintaining paperwork is easily accomplished with this menu.

Short time period. These menus are intended for shorter periods of time, between 1–3 weeks.

Limitations

Few topics. These menus only cover one or three topics.

Student compromise. Although this menu does allow choice, a student will sometimes have to compromise and complete an activity he or she would not have chosen because it completes the required tic-tac-toe. (This is not always bad, though!)

Time Considerations

These menus are usually intended for shorter amounts of completion time—at the most, they should take 3 weeks with one product submitted each week. If the menu focuses on one topic in depth, it can be completed in 1 week.

List Menu

Description

The List menu (see Figure 1.3), or Challenge List, is a more complex menu than the Tic-Tac-Toe menu, with a total of at least 10 predetermined choices, each with its own point value, and at least one free choice for students. Choices are simply listed with assigned points based on the levels of Bloom's Revised taxonomy. The choices carry different weights and have different expectations for completion time and effort. A point criterion is set forth that equals 100%, and students choose how they wish to attain that point goal.

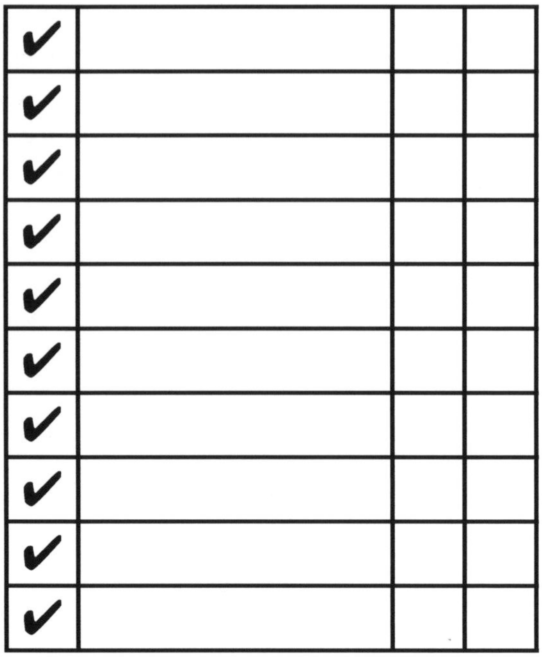

Benefits

Responsibility. Students have complete control over their grades. They really like the idea that they can guarantee their grades if they complete the required work. If they lose points on one of the chosen assignments, they can complete another to be sure they have met their goal points. This responsibility over their own grades also allows a shift in thinking about grades—whereas many students think of grades in terms of how the teacher judged their work, having control over their grades leads students to understand that they *earn* their grades.

Figure 1.3. List menu.

Different learning levels. This menu also has the flexibility to allow for individualized contracts for different learning levels within the classroom. Each student can contract for a certain number of points for his or her 100%.

Concept reinforcement. This menu allows for an in-depth study of material; however, with the different levels of Bloom's Revised taxonomy being represented, students who are still learning the concepts can choose some of the lower level point value projects to reinforce the basics before jumping into the higher level activities.

Variety. A list menu offers a larger variety of product choices. There is guaranteed to be a product of interest to everyone.

Limitations

One topic. This menu is best used for one topic in depth, so that students cannot miss any specific content.

Cannot guarantee objectives. If this menu is used for more than one topic, it is possible for a student not to have to complete an activity for each objective, depending on the choices he or she makes.

Preparation. Teachers need to have all materials ready at the beginning of the unit for students to be able to choose any of the activities on the list, which requires advanced planning. (Note: Once the materials are assembled, the menu is wonderfully low stress!)

Time Considerations

List menus are usually intended for shorter amounts of completion time—at the most, 2 weeks.

2-5-8 Menu

> "My favorite menu is the 2-5-8 kind. It's easy to understand, and I can pick just what I want to do."
>
> —Fourth-grade student, when asked about his favorite type of menu

Description

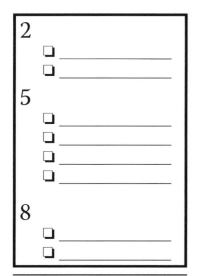

Figure 1.4. 2-5-8 menu.

A 2-5-8 menu (see Figure 1.4; Magner, 2000) is a variation of a List menu, with a total of at least eight predetermined choices: two choices with a point value of two, at least four choices with a point value of five, and at least two choices with a point value of eight. Choices are assigned points based on the levels of Bloom's Revised taxonomy. Choices with a point value of two represent the "remember" and "understand" levels, choices with a point value of five represent the "apply" and "analyze" levels, and choices with a point value of eight represent the "evaluate" and "create" levels. All levels of choices carry different weights and have different expectations for completion time and effort. Students are expected to earn 10 points for a 100%. Students choose what combination they would like to use to attain that point goal.

Benefits

Responsibility. With this menu, students still have complete control over their grades.

Low stress. This menu is one of the shortest menus, and if students choose well, they could accomplish their goal by completing only two products. This menu is usually not as daunting as some of the longer, more complex menus.

Guaranteed activity. This menu's design is also set up in such a way that students must complete at least one activity at a higher level of Bloom's Revised taxonomy in order to reach their point goal.

Limitations

One topic. Although it can be used for more than one topic, this menu works best with an in-depth study of one topic.

No free choice. By nature, this menu does not allow students to propose their own free choice, because point values need to be assigned based on Bloom's Revised taxonomy.

Higher level thinking. Students may choose to complete only one activity at a higher level of thinking.

Time Considerations

The 2-5-8 menu is usually intended for a shorter amount of completion time—at the most, 1 week.

Game Show Menu

"This menu really allowed me to compact for my students, as I have so many different levels in my classroom. As students showed me they understood new concepts, they were allowed to work on their class work and then the column of the game show menu available for that day. It was such a motivator!"

—*Fourth-grade science/math teacher*

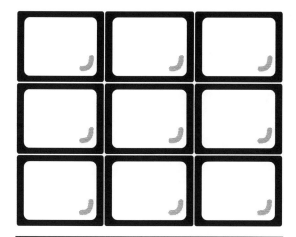

Figure 1.5. Game Show menu.

Description

The Game Show menu (see Figure 1.5) is a complex menu. It covers multiple topics or objectives with at least four predetermined choices and a free student choice for each objective. Choices are assigned points based on the levels of Bloom's Revised taxonomy. All choices carry different weights and have different expectations for completion time and effort. A point criterion is set forth that equals 100%. Students must complete at least one activity from each objective in order to reach their goal.

Benefits

Free choice. This menu allows many choices for students, but if they do not want to complete the offered activities, they can propose their own activity for each objective.

Responsibility. This menu allows students to guarantee their own grades.

Different learning levels. This menu has the flexibility to allow for individualized contracts for different learning levels within the classroom. Each student can contract for a certain number of points for his or her 100%.

Objectives guaranteed. The teacher is guaranteed that the students complete an activity from each objective covered, even if it is at a lower level.

Limitations

Confirm expectations. The only real limitation for this menu is that students (and parents) must understand the guidelines for completing the menu.

Time Considerations

These menus are usually intended for a longer amount of completion time. Although they can be used as a yearlong menu (each column could be for one grading period), they are usually intended for 2–3 weeks.

Free Choice in the Inclusive Classroom

> "Free choice? What do you mean? I don't get it."
> —*Fourth-grade student with special needs*

Most of the menus included in this book allow students to submit a free choice as a product. This free choice is a product of their choosing that addresses the content being studied and shows what the student has learned about the topic. Although this option is offered, students may not fully understand its benefits or immediately respond to the opportunity even after it has been explained. Although certain students have been offered choices before and may be very excited by the idea of taking charge of their own learning, our students with special needs may not have had much exposure to this concept. Their educational experiences tend to be objective-based and teacher-driven. This is not to say that they would not respond well to the idea of free choice; in fact, they can embrace it as enthusiastically as gifted students can. The most significant difference between these two groups successfully approaching free choice is the amount of content needed by the student before he or she embarks on a proposed option. Our students with special needs need to feel confident in their knowledge of the content and information before they are ready to step out on their own, propose their own ideas, and create their own products. Average students may be comfortable with less knowledge and structure.

With most of the menus, the students are allowed to submit a free choice for their teacher's consideration. Figure 1.6 shows two sample proposal forms that have been used many times successfully in my classroom. The form used is based on the type of menu being presented. If students are using the Tic-Tac-Toe or Three Shape menu, there is no need to submit a point proposal. A copy of these forms should be given to each student when each menu is first introduced. A discussion should be held with the students so they understand the expectations of a free choice. If students do not want to make a proposal using the proposal form after the teacher has discussed the entire menu and its activities, they can place the unused form in a designated place in the classroom. Others may want to use their form, and it is often surprising who wants to submit a proposal form after hearing about the opportunity!

Name: _____   Teacher's Approval: _____

Free-Choice Proposal Form for Point-Based Menu

Points Requested: _____   Points Approved: _____

Proposal Outline

1. What specific topic or idea will you learn about?

2. What criteria should be used to grade it? (Neatness, content, creativity, artistic value, etc.)

3. What will your product look like?

4. What materials will you need from the teacher to create this product?

Name: _____   Teacher's Approval: _____

Free-Choice Proposal Form

Proposal Outline

1. What specific topic or idea will you learn about?

2. What criteria should be used to grade it? (Neatness, content, creativity, artistic value, etc.)

3. What will your product look like?

4. What materials will you need from the teacher to create this product?

Figure 1.6. Sample proposal forms for free choice.

Proposal forms must be submitted before students begin working on their free-choice products. The teacher then knows what the students are working on, and the student knows the expectations the teacher has for that product. Once the project has been approved, the forms can easily be stapled to the student's menu sheet. The student can refer to the forms while developing the free-choice product, and when the grading takes place, the teacher can refer to the agreement for the graded features of the product.

Each part of the proposal form is important and needs to be discussed with students:

- *Name/Teacher's Approval.* The student must submit this form to the teacher for approval. The teacher will carefully review all of the information, discuss any suggestions or alterations with the student, if needed, and then sign the top.

- *Points Requested.* Found only on the point-based menu proposal form, this is where negotiation may need to take place. Students usually will submit their first request for a very high number (even the 100% goal). They tend to equate the amount of time something will take with the number of points it should earn. But please note that the points are always based on the levels of Bloom's Revised taxonomy. For example, a PowerPoint presentation with a vocabulary word quiz would get minimal points, although it may have taken a long time to create. If the students have not been exposed to the levels of Bloom's Revised taxonomy, this can be difficult to explain. You can always refer to the popular "Bloom's Verbs" to help explain the difference between time-consuming and higher level activities.

- *Points Approved.* Found only on the point-based menu proposal form, this is the final decision recorded by the teacher once the point haggling is finished.

- *Proposal Outline.* This is where the student will tell you everything about the product he or she intends to complete. These questions should be completed in such a way that you can really picture what the student is planning to complete. This also shows you that the student knows what he or she plans to complete.

  o *What specific topic or idea will you learn about?* Students need to be specific here. It is not acceptable to write "science" or "reading." This is where students look at the objectives of the project and choose which objective their project demonstrates.

  o *What criteria should be used to grade it?* Although there are rubrics for all of the projects that the students might create, it is important for the students to explain what criteria are most important to evaluate the product. The student may indicate that the rubric being used for all of the predetermined projects is fine; however, he or she may also want to add other criteria here.

o *What will your product look like?* It is important that this response be as detailed as possible. If a student cannot express what it will look like, then he or she has probably not given the free-choice plan enough thought.

o *What materials will you need from the teacher to create this product?* This is an important consideration. Sometimes students do not have the means to purchase items for their project. This can be negotiated as well, but if you ask what students may need, they will often develop even grander ideas for their free choice.

CHAPTER 2

How to Use Menus in the Inclusive Classroom

There are different ways to use instructional menus in the inclusive classroom. In order to decide how to implement each menu, the following questions should be considered: How much prior knowledge of the topic being taught do the students have before the unit or lesson begins, how confident are your students in making choices and working independently, and how much intellectually appropriate information is readily available for students to obtain on their own?

There are many ways to use menus in the classroom. One way that is often overlooked is using menus to review or build background knowledge before a unit begins. This is frequently used when students have had exposure to upcoming content in the past, perhaps during the previous year's instruction or through similar life experiences. Although they may have been exposed to the content previously, students may not remember the details of the content at the level needed to proceed with the upcoming unit immediately. A shorter menu covering the previous years' objectives can be provided in the weeks prior to the new unit so that students have the opportunity to recall and engage with the information in a meaningful way. They are then ready to take it to a deeper level during the unit. For example, 2 weeks before starting a unit on poetry, the teacher may select a short menu on Shel Silverstein or another familiar poet, knowing that the students have covered the content in the past and should be able to successfully work independently on the menu by engaging their prior knowledge. Students work on products from the menu as anchor activities and homework throughout the 2 weeks preceding the poetry unit, with all products being submitted prior to the unit's initiation. This way, the students have been in the "poetry frame of mind" independently for 2 weeks and are ready to investigate the topic further.

Introducing menus for enrichment and supplementary activities is the most common way of using menus. In this case, the students usually do not have a lot of background knowledge, and information about the topic may not be readily available to all students. The teacher will introduce the menu and the activities at the beginning of a unit. The teacher will then progress through the content at the normal rate, using his or her own curricular materials and periodically allowing class time and homework time throughout the unit for students to work on their menu choices to promote a deeper understanding of the lessons being taught. This method is very effective, as it incorporates an immediate use for the content the teacher is covering. For example, at the beginning of a unit on references, the teacher may introduce the menu with the explanation that students may not yet have all of the knowledge needed to complete all of their choices. The teacher would explain that during the unit, more content would be provided and students would be prepared to work on new choices. If students wanted to work ahead, they could certainly find the information on their own, but that would not be required. Although gifted students often see this as a challenge and begin to investigate concepts mentioned in the menu before the teacher has discussed them, other students begin to develop questions about the concepts and are ready to ask them when the teacher covers the material. This helps build an immense pool of background knowledge and possible content questions before the topic is even discussed in the classroom. As teachers, we constantly fight the battle of trying to get students to read ahead or come to class already prepared for discussion. By introducing a menu at the beginning of a unit and allowing students to complete products as instruction progresses, we encourage the students to naturally investigate the information and come to class prepared without having to make preparation a separate requirement.

Another option for using menus in the classroom is to replace certain curricular activities the teacher uses to teach the specified content. In this case, the students may have some limited background knowledge about the content and have information readily available for them among their classroom resources. This situation allows the teacher to pick and choose which aspects of the content need to be directly taught to the students in large or small groups and which can be appropriately learned and reinforced through product menus. The unit is then designed using formal instructional large-group lessons, smaller informal group lessons, and specific menu days during which the students use the menu to reinforce the prior knowledge they have already gained. In order for this option to be effective, the teacher must feel very comfortable with the students' prior knowledge level and their readiness to work independently. Another variation on this method is using the menus to drive center or station activities. Centers have many different functions in the classroom—most importantly, reinforcing the instruction that has already taken place. Rather than having a set rotation for centers, the teacher may use the menu activities as enrichment or as supplementary activities during center time for those students who need more than just reinforcement; centers can be set up with the materials students would need to complete various products.

Yet another option for menu use is the use of mini-lessons, with the menus driving the accompanying classroom activities. This method is best used when the majority of the students have similar amounts of knowledge about the topic. The teacher can design 15–20-minute mini-lessons in which students quickly review basic concepts that are already familiar to them and are then exposed to the new content in a short and concise way. Then students are turned loose to choose an activity on the menu to show that they understand the concept. The Game Show menu usually works very well with this method of instruction, as the topics across the top usually lend themselves to these mini-lessons. It is important that the students either have some prior knowledge on the content or be effective at working independently, because the lesson cycle is shorter in this use of menus. Using menus in this way does shorten the amount of time teachers have to use the guided practice step of the lesson, so all instruction and examples should be carefully selected. By using the menus in this way, the teacher avoids the one-size-fits-all independent practice portion of the lesson. If there are still a few students struggling, they can be pulled into a small-group situation while the other students work on their choices from the menu. Another important consideration is the independence level of the students. In order for this use of menus to be effective, students will need to be able to work independently for up to 20 minutes after the mini-lesson. Because students are often interested in the product they have chosen, this is not a critical issue, but it is still one worth mentioning as teachers consider how they would like to use various menus in their classroom.

Introducing and Using Leveled Menus With Students

The menus in this book are tiered versions of the menus found in its companion series, Differentiation Instruction With Menus. Although the topics and objectives are alike, these menus may have different values assigned to the same tasks, slightly different wording for similar tasks, the same product options in a menu of a different format, or even tasks that are only available on certain menus. All of these minor modifications make certain menus more appropriate for different students based on their readiness, interests, and ability levels.

As we all know, students tend to compare answers, work, and ideas, and the same goes for their menu choices. Although students may notice the slight aforementioned differences, it may not be an issue when students are working in ability groups, as students are comfortable with not having the exact same options as their classmates. It may also not be an issue when the menus are presented in a matter-of-fact manner, as everyone is getting a menu that was especially chosen for him or her, so students may notice some differences between their menus. Students should rest assured that target numbers (e.g., a goal of 100 points must be met to receive a 100%) is equal for all of the menus provided, and that the activities most often preferred by students are found on all of the menus. Students should also know that most of the menus have a free-choice proposal option, so if they really want to do one of the activities found on another menu in the classroom, they are welcome to submit a free-choice proposal form in order to complete that activity. By presenting tiered menus with confidence and by making it clear that each menu is selected specifically for each student, you can make students much more willing to accept the system and proceed within the confines that you have set.

That being said, you may still have a few students who say, in that dreaded nasal, accusatory tone, "That's still not fair!" When I first starting using leveled menus, I heard a few comments like this. They quickly dissipated with my standard and practiced responses. Of course, the first response (which they do not always appreciate) is that fair is not the same as equal. I know students do not like to hear this response, as it is patently true and therefore difficult to dispute. Secondly, I remind students that everyone has different strengths, and the menus are distributed in order to emphasize students' strengths. Again, they know this; they just do not like to acknowledge it. Lastly, if the students are being especially surly, I sometimes have to play the "parent card," meaning that I am the teacher and so have the right to do what I feel is best for each student. This last option is nonnegotiable, and although students may not like it, they understand the tone and sentiment, as they have usually experienced it at home.

The bottom line when it comes to tiered menu use is that students will respond to the use of different menus within one classroom based on how the teacher presents or reacts to it. In the past, when I have used different formats, I have addressed the format or obvious differences in a matter-of-fact manner, by saying things such as, "I have spiced things up with this menu and have three different ones that I will pass out. You may receive one that is different than your neighbor's, but whichever one you receive is going to be lots of fun for you!" Other times, when the menus are very similar in their formats and graphics, I simply distribute them and address concerns when they are brought up. For the most part, students are more likely to simply go with what they have been given when the differences in menus are presented confidently, without being open to debate or complaint.

CHAPTER 3

Guidelines for Products

"Each project is unique."

—Fifth-grade student, when asked why he enjoys choice menus

This chapter outlines the different types of products included in the featured menus, as well as the guidelines and expectations for each. It is very important that students know exactly what the expectations of a completed product are when they choose to work on it. By discussing these expectations before students begin and having the information readily available ahead of time, you will limit the frustration on everyone's part.

$1 Contract

Consideration should be given to the cost of creating the products featured on any menu. The resources available to students vary within a classroom, and students should not be graded on the amount of materials they can purchase to make a product look better. These menus are designed to equalize the resources students have available. The materials for most products are available for less than a dollar and can often be found in a teacher's classroom as part of the classroom supplies. If a product requires materials from the student, there is a $1 contract as part of the product criteria. This is a very important piece in the explanation of the product. First of all, by limiting the amount of money a child can spend, teachers create an equal amount of resources for all students. Second, this practice actually encourages a more creative product. When students are limited by the amount of materials they can readily purchase, they often have to use materials from home in new and unique ways. Figure 3.1 is a sample of the contract that has been used many times in my classroom with various products.

$1 Contract

I did not spend more than $1.00 on my _____.

_____   _____
                Student Signature   Date

My child, _____, did not spend more than $1.00 on the product he or she created.

_____   _____
                Parent Signature   Date

Figure 3.1. $1 contract.

The Products

Table 3.1 contains a list of the products used in this book. These products were chosen for their flexibility in meeting different learning styles, as well as for being products many teachers are already using in their classroom. They have been arranged by learning style—visual, kinesthetic, or auditory—and each menu has been designed to include products from all of these learning styles. Of course, some of the products may represent more than one style of learning, depending on how

Table 3.1
Products

Visual	Kinesthetic	Auditory
Acrostic	Collection	Interview
Advertisement	Commercial	News Report
Book Cover	Concentration Cards	Play
Brochure/Pamphlet	Diorama	PowerPoint—Speaker
Bumper Sticker	Flipbook	Song/Rap
Cartoon/Comic Strip	Game	Speech
Children's Book	Mobile	Student-Taught
Collage	Model	Lesson
Commercial	Play	Video
Crossword Puzzle	Product Cube	You Be the Person
Diary	Puppet/Puppet Show	Presentation
Dictionary	Science Experiment	
Drawing	Trophy	
Greeting Card	Video	
Instruction Card		
Letter		
List		
Map		
Mind Map		
Newspaper Article		
Poster		
PowerPoint—		
Stand-Alone		
Questionnaire		
Recipe/Recipe Card		
Report		
Scrapbook		
Sculpture		
Story		
Summary		
Three Facts and a Fib		
Timeline		
Trading Cards		
Venn Diagram		
Windowpane		
Worksheet		

they are presented or implemented. Some of these products are featured in the menus more often than others, but students may choose the less common products as free-choice options.

Product Frustrations

One of the biggest frustrations that accompany the use of these various products on menus is the barrage of questions about the products themselves. Students can become so wrapped up in the products and the criteria for creating them that they do not focus on the content being presented. This is especially true when menus are introduced to the class. Students can spend an exorbitant amount of time asking the teacher about the products mentioned on the menu. When this happens, what should have been a 10–15-minute menu introduction turns into 45–50 minutes of discussion about product expectations. In order to facilitate the introduction of the menu products, teachers may consider showing students examples of the product(s) from the previous year. Although this can be helpful, it can also lead to additional frustration on the part of both the teacher and the students. Some students may not feel that they can produce a product as nice, as big, as special, or as (you fill in the blank) as the example, or when shown an example, students might interpret that as meaning that the teacher would like something exactly like the one he or she showed to students. To avoid this situation, I would propose that when using examples, the example students are shown be a "blank" one that demonstrates how to create only the shell of the product. If an example of a windowpane is needed, for instance, students might be shown a blank piece of paper that is divided into six panes. The students can then take the "skeleton" of the product and make it their own as they create their own version of the windowpane using their information.

Product Guidelines

Most frustrations associated with products can be addressed proactively through the use of standardized, predetermined product guidelines, to be shared with students prior to them creating any products. These product guidelines are designed in a specific yet generic way, such that any time throughout the school year that the students select a product, that product's guidelines will apply. A beneficial side effect of using set guidelines for a product is the security it creates. Students are often reticent to try something new, as doing so requires taking a risk.

Traditionally, when students select a product, they ask questions about creating it, hope they remember and understood all of the details, and turn it in. It can be quite a surprise when they receive the product back and realize that it was not complete or was not what was expected. As you can imagine, students may not want to take the risk on something new the next time; they often prefer to do what they know and be successful. Through the use of product guidelines, students can begin to feel secure in their choice before they start working on a new product. If they are not feeling secure, they tend to stay within their comfort zone.

The product guidelines for menu products included in this book, as well as some potential free-choice options, are included in an easy-to-read card format (see Figure 3.2) with graphics that depict the guidelines and help the students remember the important criteria for each product. (The guidelines for some products, such as summaries, are omitted because teachers often have different criteria for these products.) Once the products and/or menus have been selected, there are many options available to share this information.

There really is no one "right way" to share the product guideline information with your students. It all depends on their abilities and needs. Some teachers choose to duplicate and distribute all of the product guidelines pages to students at the beginning of the year so that each child has his or her own copy while working on products. As another option, a few classroom sets can be created by gluing each product guideline card onto a separate index card, hole punching the corner of each card, and placing all of the cards on a metal ring. These ring sets can be placed in a central location or at centers where students can borrow and return them as they work on their products. This allows for the addition of products as they are introduced. Some teachers prefer to introduce product guidelines as students experience products on their menus. In this case, product guidelines from the menu currently assigned can be enlarged, laminated, and posted on a bulletin board for easy access during classroom work. Some teachers may choose to reproduce each menu's specific product guidelines on the back of the menu. No matter which method teachers choose to share the information with the students, they will save themselves a lot of time and frustration by having the product guidelines available for student reference (e.g., "Look at your product guidelines—I think that will answer your question").

Acrostic

- At least 8.5" x 11"
- Neatly written or typed
- Target word will be written down the left side of the paper
- Each descriptive word chosen must begin with one of the letters from the target word
- Each descriptive word chosen must be related to the target word

Advertisement

- At least 8.5" x 11"
- Should include a slogan
- Color picture of item or service
- Include price, if appropriate

Book Cover

- Front Cover–title, author, image
- Cover Inside Flap–summary of book
- Back Inside Flap–brief biography of author
- Back Cover–comments about book
- Spine–title and author
- May be placed on actual book, but does not have to be

Brochure/Pamphlet

- At least 8.5" x 11"
- Must be in three-fold format; front fold has title and picture
- Must have both pictures and information
- Information should be in paragraph form with at least five facts included

Figure 3.2. Product guidelines.

Bumper Sticker

- Uses a regular piece of paper cut in half lengthwise
- Must have a picture to meet the task
- Must have a motto

Cartoon/Comic Strip

- At least 8.5" x 11"
- At least six cells
- Must have meaningful dialogue
- Must have color

Children's Book

- Must have cover with book's title and author's name
- Must have at least five pages
- Each page should have an illustration to accompany the story
- Should be neatly written or typed
- Can be developed on the computer

Collage

- At least 8.5" x 11"
- Pictures must be neatly cut from magazines or newspapers (no clip art)
- Label items as required in task

Figure 3.2. Continued.

Commercial

- Must be between 2–3 minutes
- Script must be turned in before commercial is presented
- Can be presented live to an audience or recorded
- Should have props or some form of costume
- Can include more than one person

Concentration Cards

- At least 20 index cards (10 matching sets)
- Can use both pictures and words
- Information should be placed on just one side of each card
- Include an answer key that shows the matches
- All cards must be submitted in a carrying bag

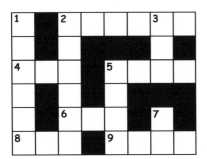

Crossword Puzzle

- Must include at least 20 significant words or phrases
- Clues must be appropriate
- Include puzzle and answer key

Diary

- Neatly written or typed
- Include appropriate number of entries
- Include date, if appropriate
- Must be written in first person

Figure 3.2. Continued.

Dictionary

- Neatly written or made on the computer
- Definition should be in students's own words
- Has a clear picture for each word
- Pictures can be drawn or from the computer

Diorama

- At least 4" x 5" x 8"
- Must be self-standing
- All interior space covered with relevant pictures and information
- Name written on back in permanent ink
- $1 contract signed
- Informational/title card attached to diorama

Drawing

- Must be at least 8.5" x 11"
- Must include color
- Must be neatly drawn by hand
- Must have title
- Name should be written on the back

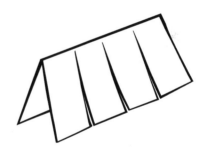

Flipbook

- At least 8.5" x 11" folded in half
- All information or opinions must be supported by facts
- Created with the correct number of flaps cut into top
- Color is optional
- Name written on the back

Figure 3.2. Continued.

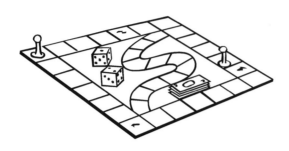

Game

- At least four thematic game pieces
- At least 25 colored/thematic squares
- At least 20 question/activity cards
- A thematic title on the board
- A complete set of rules for playing the game
- At least the size of an open file folder

Greeting Card

- Front–colored pictures, words optional
- Front Inside–personal note related to topic
- Back Inside–greeting or saying, must meet product criteria
- Back Outside–logo, publisher, and price for card

Instruction Card

- Created on heavy paper or card
- Neatly written or typed
- Uses color drawings
- Provides instructions stated

Interview

- Must have at least five questions important to topic being studied
- Questions and answers must be neatly written or typed
- Must include name of person being interviewed
- Must get teacher or parent permission before interviewing person

Figure 3.2. Continued.

Letter

- Neatly written or typed
- Must use proper letter format
- At least three paragraphs
- Must follow type of letter stated in menu (friendly, persuasive, informational)

List

- Neatly written or made on the computer
- Has the number of items required
- Is as complete as possible
- Alphabet lists need words or phrases for each letter of the alphabet except X

Map

- At least 8.5" x 11"
- Accurate information
- Must include at least 10 relevant locations
- Includes compass rose, legend, scale, key

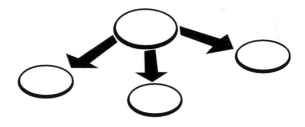

Mind Map

- At least 8.5" x 11" unlined paper
- Must have one central idea
- Follow the "no more than four rule" (there should be no more than four words coming from any one word)

Figure 3.2. Continued.

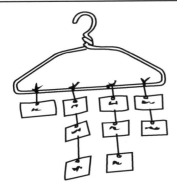

Mobile

- At least 10 pieces of related information
- Includes color and pictures
- At least three layers of hanging information
- Be able to hang in a balanced way

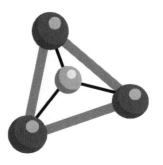

Model

- At least 8" x 8" x 12"
- Parts of model must be labeled
- Should be to scale when appropriate
- Must include a title card
- Name permanently written on model

News Report

- Must address the who, what, where, when, why, and how of topic
- Script of report turned in with project (or before if performance will be live)
- Can be either live or recorded

Newspaper Article

- Must be informational in nature
- Must follow standard newspaper format
- Must include picture with caption that supports article
- At least three paragraphs
- Neatly written or typed

Figure 3.2. Continued.

Play

- Must be between 3–5 minutes
- Script must be turned in before play is presented
- Must be presented to an audience
- Should have props or some form of costume
- Can include more than one person

Poster

- Should be size of standard poster board
- At least five pieces of important information
- Must have title
- Must have both words and pictures
- Name must be written on back

PowerPoint – Speaker

- At least 10 informational slides and one title slide with student's name
- No more than two words per page
- Slides must have color and at least one graphic per page
- Animations are optional but should not distract from information being presented
- Presentation should be timed and flow with speech being given

PowerPoint – Stand-Alone

- At least 10 informational slides and one title slide with student's name
- No more than 10 words per page
- Slides must have color and at least one graphic per page
- Animations are optional but must not distract from information being presented

Figure 3.2. Continued.

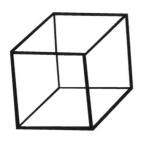

Product Cube

- All six sides of cube must be filled with information
- Name must be printed neatly on bottom of one side of cube

Puppet

- Puppet must be handmade and must have a moveable mouth
- A list of supplies used to make puppet must be turned in with puppet
- $1 contract signed
- If used in puppet show, all puppet show criteria must also be met

Puppet Show

- Must be between 3–5 minutes
- Script must be turned in before show is presented
- Must be presented to an audience
- Should have a different puppet for each role

Questionnaire

- Neatly written or typed
- At least 10 questions with possible answers
- At least one answer that requires a written response
- Questions must be related to topic being studied

Figure 3.2. Continued.

Recipe/Recipe Card

- Must be written neatly or typed on a piece of paper or index card
- Must have list of ingredients with measurements for each
- Must have numbered steps that explain how to make the recipe

Report

- Neatly written or made on the computer
- Must have enough information to address topic
- Information has to be student's own words, not copied from a book or the Internet

Scrapbook

- Cover of scrapbook must have meaningful title and student's name
- Must have at least five themed pages
- Each page must have at least one picture
- All photos must have captions

Sculpture

- Cannot be larger than 2 feet tall
- Must include any specified items
- Name should be written on bottom
- Must not use any valuable materials

Figure 3.2. Continued.

Song/Rap

- Words must make sense
- Can be presented to an audience or recorded
- Written words will be turned in
- Should be at least 1 minute in length

Speech

- Must be at least 2 minutes in length
- Should not be read from written paper
- Note cards can be used
- Written speech must be turned in
- Voice must be clear, loud, and easy to understand

Story

- Must be neatly written or typed
- Must have all elements of a well-written story (setting, characters, problem, events, resolution)
- Must be appropriate length to allow for story elements

Three Facts and a Fib

- Can be written, typed, or created using Microsoft PowerPoint
- Must include exactly four statements: three true statements and one false statement
- False statement should not obvious
- Brief paragraph should be included that explains why the fib is false

Figure 3.2. Continued.

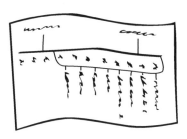

Timeline

- No bigger than standard-sized poster board
- Must be divided into equal intervals of time
- Must contain at least 10 important dates
- Must have an explanation of at least two sentences for each date about its importance

Trading Cards

- Include at least 10 cards
- Each card should be at least 3" x 5"
- Each should have a colored picture
- At least three facts on the subject of the card
- Cards must have information on both sides
- All cards must be submitted in a carrying bag

Trophy

- Must be at least 6 inches tall
- Must have a base with the winner's name and the name of the award written neatly or typed on it
- Top of trophy must be appropriate to the award
- Name should be written on the bottom of the award
- Must be an originally designed trophy (avoid reusing a trophy from home)

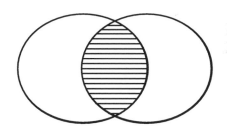

Venn Diagram

- At least 8.5" x 11"
- Shapes should be thematic and neatly drawn
- Must have a title for entire diagram and a title for each section
- Must have at least six items in each section of diagram
- Name must be written on back

Figure 3.2. Continued.

Video

- Must be recorded
- Must turn in written plan or storyboard with project
- Student must arrange to use own video recorder or allow teacher at least 3 days' notice for use of recorder
- Must cover important information about the project
- Name must be written on video or disc

Windowpane

- At least 8.5" x 11" unlined paper
- At least six squares
- Each square must include a picture and words
- Name should be recorded on bottom right-hand corner of front

Worksheet

- Must be 8.5" x 11"
- Neatly written or typed
- Must cover specific topic or question in detail
- Must be creative in design
- Must have at least one graphic
- Must turn in corresponding answer key

You Be the Person Presentation

- Take on the role of the person
- Cover at least five important facts about the life of the person
- Should be between 2–4 minutes in length
- Script must be turned in before information is presented
- Should present to an audience and answer questions while staying in character
- Must have props or some form of costume

Figure 3.2. Continued.

One of the most commonly used products in a language arts classroom is the story map. The story map is a quick and effective way for a student to dissect a story and show that he or she can analyze the important parts of that story. Story maps are an option for approximately a third of the menus provided in this book. Two examples are offered (see Figures 3.3 and 3.4), which can be used with the different menu levels as appropriate, but teachers who already use their own story map formats with students should feel free to continue using them.

Story Map

Title:_____

_____

Author: _____

Illustrator: _____

Setting of Story

_____

_____

_____

_____

_____

_____

Characters in Story
Write each character's name and give a description of the character.

_____

_____

_____

_____

Events in Story
Write all of the important events in the story, in order.

_____

_____

_____

_____

_____

_____

Figure 3.3. Basic story map.

Story Map

Title and Author	Setting

Main Characters
Write at least three traits for each character.

Supporting Characters
Write one sentence about why each is important to the story.

Problem

Major Events

Solution

Figure 3.4. Story map 2.

CHAPTER 4

Rubrics

> "All the grading of the projects kept me from using menus before. The rubric makes it easier, though, and [the different projects] are fun to see."
>
> —Fourth-grade teacher, when asked to explain reservations about using menus

The most common reason teachers feel uncomfortable with menus is the need for equal grading. Teachers often feel that it is easier to grade the same type of product made by all of the students than to grade a large number of different products, none of which looks like any other. The great equalizer for hundreds of different products is a generic rubric that can cover all of the important qualities of an excellent product.

All-Purpose Rubric

Figure 4.1 is an example of a rubric that has been classroom tested with various menus. This rubric can be used with any point value activity presented in a menu, as there are five criteria and the columns represent full points, half points, and no points.

There are different ways that this rubric can be shared with students. Some teachers prefer to provide it when a menu is presented to students. The rubric can be reproduced on the back of the menu along with its guidelines. The rubric can also be given to students to keep in their folders with their product guideline cards so they always know the expectations as they complete projects throughout the school year. Some teachers prefer to keep a master copy for themselves and post an enlarged copy of the rubric on a bulletin board, or provide one copy for parents during open house so that they understand how their children's menu products will be graded.

No matter how the rubric is shared with students, the first time they see this rubric, it should be explained to them in detail, especially the last column, titled "Self." It is very important that students self-evaluate their projects. This column can provide a unique perspective on the project as it is being graded. Note: This rubric was designed to be specific enough that students will understand the criteria the teacher is seeking, but general enough that they can still be as creative as they like while making their products.

Student Presentation Rubric

Although the all-purpose rubric can be used for all activities, there is one occasion that seems to warrant a special rubric: student presentations. A student presentation can be a unique situation with many details that should be considered separately.

Student presentations can be difficult to evaluate. With these types of presentations, objectivity must be the first consideration. The objectivity can be addressed through a very specific presentation rubric that states what is expected of the speaker. The rubric will need to be discussed and various criteria demonstrated before the students begin preparing presentations. The second consideration is that of the audience and its interest. How frustrating it can be to grade 30 presentations when the audience is not paying attention! This issue can be solved by allowing your audience to be directly involved in the presentation. Once all of

Name: _____

All-Purpose Product Rubric

	☺ **Excellent** (Full Points)	☺ **Good** (Half Points)	☹ **Poor** (No Points)	**Self**
Completeness Is everything included in the product?	All information needed is included. Meets product guidelines.	Some important information is missing. Meets product guidelines.	Most important information is missing or does not meet guidelines.	
Creativity Is the product original?	Information is creative. Graphics are original. Presentations are unique.	Information is creative. Graphics are not original or were found on the computer.	There is no evidence of new thoughts or perspectives in the product.	
Correctness Is all the information included correct?	All information in the product is correct.		Any portion of the information included is incorrect.	
Appropriate Communication Is the information well communicated?	All information is neat, easy to read, or—if presented— easy to understand.	Most of the product is neat, easy to read, and—if presented— easy to understand.	The product is not neat or is not easy to read.	
Effort and Time Did student put significant effort into the product?	Effort is obvious.		The product does not show significant effort.	

Figure 4.1. All-purpose product rubric.

the students have been familiarized with the student presentation rubric (see Figure 4.2), when they receive their own rubrics with which to give feedback to their classmates (see Figure 4.3), they are quite comfortable with the criteria. Students are asked to rank their classmates on a scale of 1–10 in the areas of content, flow, and the prop chosen to enhance the presentation. They are also asked to state two things the presenter did well. Although most students understand that this should be a positive experience for the presenter, you may want to review guidelines for what students should *not* include in their feedback. For example, if the presenter dropped his or her product and had to pick it up, then the presenter already knows this; it does not need to be noted again. The feedback should be positive and specific. Rather than writing, "Great job," a student should write something specific, such as, "I could hear you speak loudly and clearly throughout the entire presentation," or, "You had great graphics!" These types of comments really make the students take note of areas where they could improve and feel great about their presentations. The teacher should not be surprised to note that the students often look through all of their classmates' feedback and comments before ever consulting the rubric completed by the teacher. Once students have completed feedback forms for a presenter, the forms can then be gathered at the end of each presentation, stapled together, and given to the presenter at the end of the class.

Name: _____

Student Presentation Rubric

	Excellent	Good	Fair	Poor	Self
Content Complete Did the presentation include everything it should?	**30** Presentation included all important information about topic being presented.	**20** Presentation covered most of the important information, but one key idea was missing.	**10** Presentation covered some of the important information, but more than one key idea was missing.	**0** Presentation covered information, but the information was trivial or fluff.	
Content Correct Was the information presented accurate?	**30** All information presented was accurate.	**20** All information presented was correct, with a few unintentional errors that were quickly corrected.	Not applicable: There is no middle ground when it comes to correctness of content.	**0** Any information presented was not correct.	
Prop Did the speaker have at least one prop that was directly related to the presentation?	**20** Presenter had a prop and it complemented the presentation.	**12** Presenter had a prop, but it was not the best choice.	**4** Presenter had a prop, but there was no clear reason for it.	**0** Presenter had no prop.	
Content Consistent Did the speaker stay on topic?	**10** Presenter stayed on topic 100% of the time.	**7** Presenter stayed on topic 90–99% of the time.	**4** Presenter stayed on topic 80–89% of the time.	**0** It was hard to tell what the topic was.	
Flow Was the speaker familiar and comfortable with the material so that it flowed well?	**10** Presentation flowed well. Speaker did not stumble over words.	**7** Presenter had some flow problems, but they did not distract from information.	**4** Some flow problems interrupted the presentation, and presenter seemed flustered.	**0** Constant flow problems occurred, and information was not presented so that it could be understood.	
				Total Grade:	

Figure 4.2. Student presentation rubric.

Topic: _____ **Student's Name:** _____

On a scale of 1–10, rate the following areas:

Content (How in depth was the information? How well did the speaker know the information? Was the information correct? Could the speaker answer questions?)		Give one short reason why you gave this number.
Flow (Did the presentation flow smoothly? Did the speaker appear confident and ready to speak?)		Give one short reason why you gave this number.
Prop (Did the speaker explain his or her prop? Did this choice seem logical? Was it the best choice?)		Give one short reason why you gave this number.

Comments: Below, write two things that you think the presenter did well:

1. _____

_____

2. _____

_____

- -

Topic: _____ **Student's Name:** _____

On a scale of 1–10, rate the following areas:

Content (How in depth was the information? How well did the speaker know the information? Was the information correct? Could the speaker answer questions?)		Give one short reason why you gave this number.
Flow (Did the presentation flow smoothly? Did the speaker appear confident and ready to speak?)		Give one short reason why you gave this number.
Prop (Did the speaker explain his or her prop? Did this choice seem logical? Was it the best choice?)		Give one short reason why you gave this number.

Comments: Below, write two things that you think the presenter did well:

1. _____

_____

2. _____

_____

Figure 4.3. Student feedback form.

The Menus

How to Use the Menu Pages

Each menu in this section has:
- an introduction page for the teacher;
- a lower level content menu, indicated by a triangle (▲) in the upper right-hand corner;
- a middle-level content menu, indicated by a circle (●) in the upper right-hand corner;
- any specific guidelines for the menu; and
- activities mentioned in the menu.

Introduction Pages

The introduction pages are meant to provide an overview of each menu. They are divided into five areas:

1. *Objectives Covered Through These Menus and These Activities.* This area will list all of the objectives that the menus can address. Menus are arranged in such a way that if students complete the guidelines set forth in the instructions for the menus, all of these objectives will be covered.

2. *Materials Needed by Students for Completion.* For each menu, it is expected that the teacher will provide, or students will have access to, the following materials:
   - lined paper;
   - glue;
   - crayons, colored pencils, or markers; and
   - blank 8.5" x 11" white paper.

   The introduction page also includes a list of additional materials that may be needed by students as they complete either menu. Any materials listed that are used in only one of the two menus are designated with the menu's corresponding code (either triangle or circle). Students do have the choice about the menu items they can complete, so it is possible that the teacher will not need all of these materials for every student.

3. *Special Notes on the Use of These Menus.* Some menus allow students to choose to present demonstrations, experiments, songs, or PowerPoint presentations to their classmates. This section will give any special tips on managing these student presentations. This section will also share any tips to consider for a specific activity.

4. *Time Frame.* Most menus are best used in at least a 1-week time frame. Some are better suited to more than 2 weeks. This section will give an overview about the best time frame for completing the entire menu, as well as options for shorter time periods. If teachers do not have time to devote to an entire menu, they can certainly choose the 1–2-day option for any menu topic students are currently studying.

5. *Suggested Forms.* This is a list of the rubrics, templates, and reproducibles that should be available for students as the menus are introduced. If a menu has a free-choice option, the appropriate proposal form also will be listed here.

CHAPTER 5

Reading

My Book Report

List Menus

Reading Objectives Covered Through These Menus and These Activities

- Students will represent textual evidence and use it to prove conclusions.
- Students will make predictions based on what is read.
- Students will show comprehension by retelling or acting out events in a story.
- Students will analyze characters, their relationships, and their importance in the story.
- Students will recognize and analyze plot and problem resolution.

Writing Objectives Covered Through These Menus and These Activities

- Students will write to express their feelings, develop opinions, reflect, or problem solve.
- Students will support their responses with textual evidence.
- Students will write to inform, explain, describe, or narrate.
- Students will write to influence or persuade.

Materials Needed by Students for Completion

- Poster board or large white paper
- Shoe boxes (for dioramas)
- Blank index cards (for trading cards)
- Product cube template
- Materials for board games (e.g., folders, colored cards)
- Paper bags and socks (for puppets)
- Materials for three-dimensional timelines
- Story map of teacher's choice

Special Notes on the Use of These Menus

When it comes to book reports, there are many options available; these menus allow students some choice in what they would like to present when they share information about their books. These menus are also a great choice when having small groups of students work in literature groups. Each group's members can work together on their 100-point goal and present their book products to their classmates.

Time Frame

- 1–2 weeks—Students are given the menus as they begin to read their books, and the guidelines and point expectations are discussed. The teacher will go over all of the options on the menu and have students place check marks in the boxes next to the activities they are most interested in completing. As reading continues, the activities completed by the students can be kept until their book report presentations.
- 1–2 days—The teacher chooses an activity from an objective to use with the entire class during that lesson time.

Suggested Forms

- All-purpose rubric
- Student presentation rubric
- Point-based free-choice proposal form

Name: _____ ▲

My Book Report: Side 1

Directions: You are going to create a book report to share with the class. Everyone's report will look different, because you will be able to choose what you would like to include when sharing your book.

Guidelines:
1. You must choose **one** 50-point presentation option (Side 2) for your report.
2. You may complete as many of the activities for your book report as you like.
3. You may choose any combination of activities.
4. Your goal is 100 points. You may earn up to _____ points of extra credit.
5. You may be as creative as you like within the guidelines listed below.
6. You must show your plan to your teacher by _____.

Plan to Do	Activity to Complete (Side 1: 15–30 points)	Point Value	Date Completed	Points Earned
	Choose one of the characters in your book and make an acrostic with his or her name, using information about his or her personality.	15		
	Complete a story map for your story.	15		
	Create a diorama of your favorite scene in the story.	20		
	Create an advertisement to encourage your classmates to read your novel. Make it unique and interesting!	20		
	Create a book cover for your book.	20		
	Create a Venn diagram to compare and contrast two characters in your book.	20		
	Create a set of trading cards for all of the characters in the story (not all of them must be human!).	20		
	Complete this statement with just one word: "Everyone thinks the main character of my novel is _____." Create a cube with the six best quotes from your novel that prove your statement is true.	25		
	The Book Hall of Fame is taking nominations for the best fiction ever written. Create a nomination video for your book. Describe your book and explain why it deserves the honor.	30		
	Create a board game about your book in which players experience what your book's characters experienced as they play the game.	30		
	Create a three-dimensional timeline for the main character in your novel. Include at least one date before the novel begins.	30		
	Total number of points you are planning to earn from Side 1.	**Total points earned from Side 1:**		

My Book Report: Side 2 (Presentation Option)

Directions: You are going to create a book report to share with the class. Everyone's report will look different, because you will be able to choose what you would like to include when sharing your book.

Guidelines:

1. You must choose **one** 50-point presentation option (Side 2) for your report.
2. You may complete as many of the activities for your book report as you like.
3. You may choose any combination of activities.
4. Your goal is 100 points. You may earn up to _____ points of extra credit.
5. You may be as creative as you like within the guidelines listed below.
6. You must show your plan to your teacher by _____.

Plan to Do	Presentation Options (Side 2: 50 points)	Point Value	Date Completed	Points Earned
	Prepare a You be the Person presentation in which you come to class as one of the characters in your book. You will tell a little bit about yourself and discuss how your life was impacted by the plot of the book.	50		
	Choose one of the important events in your book and present a live news report about the event. Be sure to discuss the events that have led up to the incredible event you are covering!	50		
	Prepare a You be the Person presentation in which you come to class as the author of your book. You will tell a little bit about yourself and discuss why you wrote the book.	50		
	There are various reasons why people choose which books they would like to read. Create a live persuasive commercial that shares information about your book to encourage other people to read it. Do not give away the ending!	50		
	Create a puppet for each character in your book. Have your puppets speak about their importance to the plot of the book you read.	50		
	Free choice: must be outlined on a proposal form and approved before beginning work.	50		
	Total number of points you are planning to earn from Side 1.	**Total points earned from Side 1:**		
	Total number of points you are planning to earn from Side 2.	**Total points earned from Side 2:**		
		Grand Total (/100)		

I am planning to complete _____ activities that could earn up to a total of _____ points.

Teacher's initials _____ Student's signature _____

Name: _____

My Book Report: Side 1

Directions: You are going to create a book report to share with the class. Everyone's report will look different, because you will be able to choose what you would like to include when sharing your book.

Guidelines:

1. You must choose **one** 50-point presentation option (Side 2) for your report.
2. You may complete as many of the activities for your book report as you like.
3. You may choose any combination of activities.
4. Your goal is 100 points. You may earn up to _____ points of extra credit.
5. You may be as creative as you like within the guidelines listed below.
6. You must show your plan to your teacher by _____.

Plan to Do	Activity to Complete (Side 1: 15–25 points)	Point Value	Date Completed	Points Earned
	Choose two of the characters in your book and make an acrostic with their names, using information about their personalities.	15		
	Create a diorama of your favorite scene in the story.	15		
	Complete a story map for your story.	15		
	Create an advertisement to encourage your classmates to read your novel. Make it unique and interesting!	20		
	Create a book cover for your book.	20		
	Create a Venn diagram to compare and contrast two characters in your book.	20		
	Create a set of trading cards for all of the characters in the story (not all of them must be human!).	20		
	Complete this statement with just one word: "Everyone thinks the main character of my novel is _____." Create a cube with the six best quotes from your novel that prove that your statement is true.	25		
	The Book Hall of Fame is taking nominations for the best fiction ever written. Create a nomination video for your book. Describe your book and why it deserves the honor.	25		
	Create a board game about your book in which players experience what your book's characters experienced as they play the game.	25		
	Create a three-dimensional timeline for the main character in your novel. Include at least one date before the novel begins.	25		
	Free choice: must be outlined on a proposal form and approved before beginning work.	15–25 points		
	Total number of points you are planning to earn from Side 1.	**Total points earned from Side 1:**		

© Prufrock Press Inc. • *Differentiating Instruction With Menus for the Inclusive Classroom: Language Arts • Grades 3–5*

Name: _____   ●

My Book Report: Side 2 (Presentation Option)

Directions: You are going to create a book report to share with the class. Everyone's report will look different, because you will be able to choose what you would like to include when sharing your book.

Guidelines:

1. You must choose **one** 50-point presentation option (Side 2) for your report.
2. You may complete as many of the activities for your book report as you like.
3. You may choose any combination of activities.
4. Your goal is 100 points. You may earn up to _____ points of extra credit.
5. You may be as creative as you like within the guidelines listed below.
6. You must show your plan to your teacher by _____.

Plan to Do	Presentation Options (Side 2: 50 points)	Point Value	Date Completed	Points Earned
	Prepare a You Be the Person Presentation in which you come to class as one of the characters in your book. You will tell a little bit about yourself and discuss how your life was impacted by the plot of the book.	50		
	Choose one of the important events in your book and present a live news report about the event. Be sure to discuss the events that have led up to the incredible event you are covering!	50		
	Prepare a You be the Person Presentation in which you come to class as the author of your book. You will tell a little bit about yourself and discuss why you wrote the book.	50		
	There are various reasons why people choose which books they would like to read. Create a live persuasive commercial that shares information about your book to encourage other people to read it. Do not give away the ending!	50		
	Create puppets for each character in your book. Have your puppets speak about their importance to the plot of the book you read.	50		
	Free choice: must be outlined on a proposal form and approved before beginning work.	50		
	Total number of points you are planning to earn from Side 1.	**Total points earned from Side 1:**		
	Total number of points you are planning to earn from Side 2.	**Total points earned from Side 2:**		
		Grand Total (/100)		

I am planning to complete _____ activities that could earn up to a total of _____ points.

Teacher's initials _____ Student's signature _____

My Book Report Cube

Think about the following sentence: Everyone thinks my main character is _____. Read through your book and put a quote from the story on each side of the cube to support the statement you made with your chosen word.

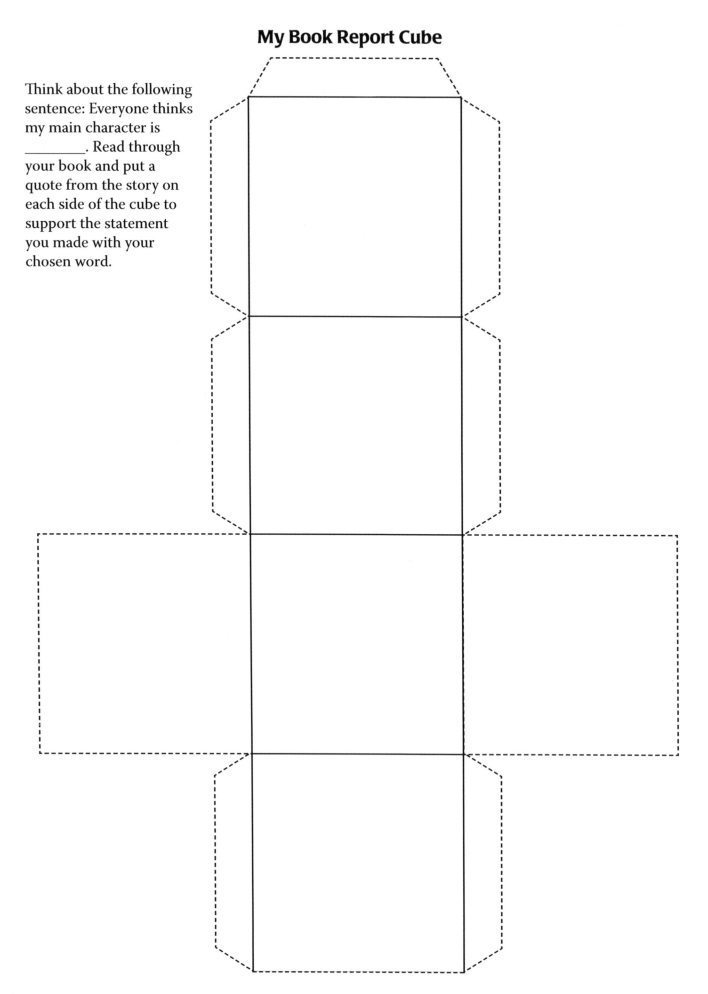

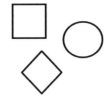

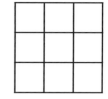

Story Elements

Three Shape Menu ▲ and Tic-Tac-Toe Menu ●

Reading Objectives Covered Through These Menus and These Activities
- Students will compare one literary work with another.
- Students will analyze various story elements, including setting, character, and plot.
- Students will draw conclusions and make predictions about what is read in the story.

Writing Objectives Covered Through These Menus and These Activities
- Students will write to express their feelings, develop opinions, reflect, or problem solve.
- Students will write to inform, explain, describe, or narrate.
- Students will write to entertain.
- Students will exhibit voice in their writing.

Materials Needed by Students for Completion
- Shoe boxes (for dioramas)
- Index cards (for trading cards)
- Magazines (for collages)
- Materials for three-dimensional timelines

Special Notes on the Use of These Menus
This topic has two different menu formats: Three Shape menu and Tic-Tac-Toe menu. The Three Shape menu is specifically selected for the triangle (lower level) option, as it easily allows the menu to be broken into manageable bits. The menu itself can be cut into strips of the same shape. Students can then be given a strip of square product choices for their use. Once they have chosen and submitted the square product for grading, they can be given the circle strip, and lastly, they can complete the diamond strip. Because this type of menu is designed to become more advanced as students move through the shapes, teachers may choose to provide their students who have special needs with the top two shapes and save the diamonds for enrichment.

Time Frame

- 2 weeks—Students are given the menus as the unit is started. The teacher will go over all of the options for that content and have students note the activities they are most interested in completing. As the teacher presents lessons throughout the week, he or she should refer back to the options associated with that content. If students are using the Tic-Tac-Toe menu form, completed products should make a column or a row. If students are using the Three Shape menu form, they should complete one product from each different shape group. When students complete these patterns, they will have completed one activity from three different objectives, learning styles, or levels of Bloom's Revised taxonomy.

- 1 week—At the start of the unit, the teacher chooses the three activities he or she feels are most valuable for the students. Stations can be set up in the classroom. These three activities are available for student choice throughout the week, as regular instruction takes place.

- 1–2 days—The teacher chooses an activity from the menus to use with the entire class.

Suggested Forms

- All-purpose rubric
- Free-choice proposal form
- Student presentation rubric

Story Elements

Directions: Choose one activity from each shape group. Circle one choice from each group of shapes. Color in the shape after you have finished it. All activities must be completed by: _____.

Create a song or rap that tells about the setting of the story.

Design a diorama that shows one of your characters in the setting of the story.

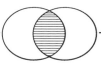

Create a Venn diagram to compare and contrast the setting from this story with the setting of another story you have read this year.

Create a set of trading cards for the characters in your book or story.

Make one acrostic for the names of two of your characters. Include words to describe each character.

Make a collage of at least 15 words and pictures that represent your main character. Be sure to place the character's name at the top.

Create a three-dimensional timeline that shows the events of your book or story.

Make a windowpane that details all of the events in your story.

Choose the most important event in the story. Write a letter that your main character may have written to his or her family to talk about the event.

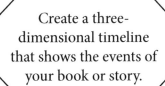

Story Elements

Directions: Check the boxes you plan to complete. They should form a tic-tac-toe across or down. All products are due by: _____.

☐ *The Setting* Create a Venn diagram to compare and contrast the setting from this story with the setting of another story you have read.	☐ *The Events* Create a three-dimensional timeline that shows the events of your book or story.	☐ *The Characters* Make a collage of at least 20 words and pictures that represent your main character. Be sure to place the character's name at the top.
☐ *The Characters* Create a set of trading cards for the characters in your book or story.	☐ **Free Choice** (Fill out your proposal form before beginning the free choice!)	☐ *The Events* Choose the most important event in your story and rewrite the rest of the story as if that event had not happened.
☐ *The Events* Make a windowpane that details all of the events in your story.	☐ *The Characters* Make one acrostic for each of your characters' names. Include words to describe each character.	☐ *The Setting* Design a diorama that shows one of your characters in the setting of the story.

Fiction

2-5-8 Menus

Reading Objectives Covered Through These Menus and These Activities
- Students will read from a variety of genres for pleasure and to acquire information.
- Students will show comprehension by summarizing the story.
- Students will analyze characters, their relationships, and their importance in the story.
- Students will recognize story problems and plot.
- Students will represent textual information by using story maps.

Writing Objectives Covered Through These Menus and These Activities
- Students will support their responses with textual evidence.
- Students will write to inform, explain, describe, or narrate.
- Students will exhibit voice in their writing.

Materials Needed by Students for Completion
- Poster board or large white paper
- Blank index cards (for recipe cards)
- Coat hangers (for mobiles)
- Index cards (for mobiles)
- String (for mobiles)
- Paper bags or socks (for puppets)
- Story map of teacher's choice

Time Frame
- 1–2 weeks—Students are given the menus as the unit is started, and the teacher discusses all of the product options on the menus. As the different options are discussed, students will choose products that add up to a total of 10 points. As the lessons progress through the week, the teacher and students refer back to the options associated with the content being taught.
- 1–2 days—The teacher chooses an activity from the menus to use with the entire class.

Suggested Forms
- All-purpose rubric
- Point-based free-choice proposal form
- Student presentation rubric

Fiction

Directions: Choose at least two activities from the menu below. The activities must total at least 10 points. Place a check mark next to each box to show which activities you will complete. All activities must be completed by:_____.

2 Points

❑ Make a mobile that shows at least three ways to tell if a story is fiction.

❑ Create a worksheet about the elements that a fictional story should contain.

5 Points

❑ Complete a story map for a fictional story of your choice.

❑ Make a recipe for a good fictional story.

❑ Create a poster to show your favorite fictional character. On the poster, place the character in his or her setting, and surround the character with elements from the story.

❑ Free choice—Prepare a proposal form and submit it to your teacher for approval.

8 Points

❑ Write your own fictional short story about someone your age and a problem that he or she must solve.

❑ Design a puppet from your favorite fictional story. Have your puppet talk about the book and share why it feels that its story should be everyone's favorite.

Name: _____

Fiction

Directions: Choose at least two activities from the menu below. The activities must total at least 10 points. Place a check mark next to each box to show which activities you will complete. All activities must be completed by:

_____.

2 Points
❐ Complete a story map for a fictional story of your choice.
❐ Make a mobile that shows at least five ways to tell if a book is fiction.

5 Points
❐ Make a recipe card for a good fictional story.
❐ Design a puppet for one of the characters in your book. Your puppet should be ready to talk about its experiences in the story.
❐ Create a poster that shows your favorite fictional character. On the poster, place the character in his or her setting, and surround the character with elements from the story.
❐ Free choice—Prepare a proposal form and submit it to your teacher for approval.

8 Points
❐ Write your own fictional short story about someone your age and a problem that he or she must solve.
❐ The Book Hall of Fame is taking nominations for the best fictional book ever written. Write a submission for this honor. Describe the book you picked and why it deserves the honor.

Tall Tales

2-5-8 Menus

Background Information

All tall tales have similar elements. See the Appendix for a book list of popular tall tales. Tall tales usually include:

*   lots of action and exaggerations,
*   a main character who faces problems and has to solve them before the end of the tale,
*   a main character who is larger than life or has superhuman abilities, and
*   a tale or piece that is funny.

Reading Objectives Covered Through These Menus and These Activities

*   Students will read from a variety of genres for pleasure and to acquire information.
*   Students will distinguish fact from fiction.
*   Students will interpret figurative language.
*   Students will recognize distinguishing features of tall tales.

Writing Objectives Covered Through These Menus and These Activities

*   Students will support their responses with textual evidence.
*   Students will write to inform, explain, describe, or narrate.
*   Students will write to entertain.
*   Students will exhibit voice and vivid language in their writing.

Materials Needed by Students for Completion

*   Video camera (for news reports)
*   Blank index cards (for trading cards)
*   Scrapbooking materials

Time Frame

*   1–2 weeks—Students are given the menus as the unit is started, and the teacher discusses all of the product options on the menus. As the different options are discussed, students will choose products that add up to a total of 10 points. As the lessons progress through the

week, the teacher and students refer back to the options associated with the content being taught.

- 1–2 days—The teacher chooses an activity from the menus to use with the entire class.

Suggested Forms

- All-purpose rubric
- Student presentation rubric

Name: _____

Tall Tales

Directions: Choose at least two activities from the menu below. The activities must total at least 10 points. Place a check mark next to each box to show which activities you will complete. All activities must be completed by:_____.

---

2 Points
- ❏ Make a mind map to show the important elements found in tall tales.
- ❏ Make a set of trading cards for characters in at least three tall tales.

---

5 Points
- ❏ Research the character in your tall tale, and create a Venn diagram to compare and contrast the fact and fiction parts of the tale.
- ❏ Perform a song or rap about the accomplishments of the main character in your tall tale.
- ❏ Design an advertisement for your main character and his or her superior skills.
- ❏ Make a scrapbook that shows the great accomplishments of the main character of your tall tale.

---

8 Points
- ❏ Create a news report to tell of the mighty accomplishments of the main character in your tall tale.
- ❏ Come to class as your favorite tall tale hero. Be prepared to tell a tale of an adventure that your classmates may not know.

Name: _____

Tall Tales

Directions: Choose at least two activities from the menu below. The activities must total at least 10 points. Place a check mark next to each box to show which activities you will complete. All activities must be completed by: _____.

---

2 Points
❏ Make a mind map to show the important elements found in tall tales.
❏ Make a set of trading cards for characters in at least five tall tales.

---

5 Points
❏ Research the character in your tall tale, and create a Venn diagram to compare and contrast the fact and fiction parts of the tale.
❏ Many songs have been sung about people who are larger than life. Find a song that tells a tall tale. Share it with the class and explain why you chose it.
❏ Design an advertisement for your main character and his or her superior skills.
❏ Make a scrapbook that shows the great accomplishments of the main character of your tall tale.

---

8 Points
❏ Pretend you are a character in your own tall tale. Write three journal entries that tell about your adventures.
❏ Come to class as your favorite tall tale hero. Be prepared to tell a tale of an adventure that your classmates may not know.

Fairy Tales

List Menus

Reading Objectives Covered Through These Menus and These Activities

- Students will prove conclusions using textual evidence.
- Students will compare literary works and genres.
- Students will show comprehension by retelling or acting out events in a story.
- Students will represent textual evidence by using story maps.

Writing Objectives Covered Through These Menus and These Activities

- Students will write to express their feelings, develop opinions, and reflect.
- Students will write to inform, explain, describe, or narrate.
- Students will write to entertain.
- Students will exhibit voice and vivid writing.

Materials Needed by Students for Completion

- Shoe boxes (for dioramas)
- Microsoft PowerPoint or other slideshow software
- Materials for board games (e.g., folders, colored cards)
- Coat hangers (for mobiles)
- Index cards (for mobiles)
- String (for mobiles)
- Graph paper or Internet access (for crossword puzzles)
- Video camera (optional for news reports)
- Materials for three-dimensional timelines
- Scrapbooking materials
- Poster board or large white paper
- Socks (for puppets)
- Paper bags (for puppets)
- Story map of teacher's choice

Time Frame

- 1–2 weeks—Students are given the menus as the unit is started, and the guidelines and point expectations are discussed. Because these menus cover one topic in depth, the teacher will go over all of the options on the menus and have students place check marks in the boxes next to the activities they are most interested in completing. As instruction continues, the activities are completed by students and submitted for grading.

- 1–2 days—The teacher chooses an activity from an objective to use with the entire class during that lesson time.

Suggested Forms

- All-purpose rubric
- Point-based free-choice proposal form

Name: _____ ▲

Fairy Tales: Side 1

Guidelines:

1. You may complete as many of the activities listed within the time period.
2. You may choose any combination of activities.
3. Your goal is 100 points. You may earn up to _____ points extra credit.
4. You may be as creative as you like within the guidelines listed below.
5. You must show your plan to your teacher by _____.
6. Activities may be turned in at any time during the working time period. They will be graded and recorded on this sheet as you continue to work, so keep it safe!

Plan to Do	Activity to Complete (Side 1: 15–30 points)	Point Value	Date Completed	Points Earned
	Complete a story map for your fairy tale.	15		
	Complete another student's crossword puzzle.	15		
	Create a character mobile to show the characters in your fairy tale. Be sure to include information about each.	20		
	Choose an important character (other than the main character) in your fairy tale and make a puppet for that character.	20		
	Create a diorama of your favorite scene from your fairy tale.	20		
	Create a crossword puzzle with information from your fairy tale.	25		
	Create a three-dimensional timeline that shows all of the events in your fairy tale.	25		
	The main character has a lot of adventures in your fairy tale. Make a scrapbook to show his or her experiences.	25		
	Draw a map to show all of the important places in your fairy tale.	25		
	Choose a job that one of the characters in your fairy tale does. Create an advertisement for the job.	25		
	Write three facts and a fib about the villain in your fairy tale.	25		
	Read two different versions of your fairy tale. Use a Venn diagram to compare and contrast them.	30		
	Total number of points you are planning to earn from Side 1.	**Total points earned from Side 1:**		

Fairy Tales: Side 2

Guidelines:

1. You may complete as many of the activities listed within the time period.
2. You may choose any combination of activities.
3. Your goal is 100 points. You may earn up to _____ points extra credit.
4. You may be as creative as you like within the guidelines listed below.
5. You must show your plan to your teacher by _____.
6. Activities may be turned in at any time during the working time period. They will be graded and recorded on this sheet as you continue to work, so keep it safe!

Plan to Do	Activity to Complete (Side 2: 35–40 points)	Point Value	Date Completed	Points Earned
	Turn your fairy tale into a board game.	35		
	Prepare a news report that tells about the most important thing that happens in your fairy tale.	35		
	Most fairy tales have an object that plays an important role. Make a model of the object in your fairy tale. Label its important parts.	35		
	Write at least three diary entries for one character in your fairy tale.	35		
	Turn your fairy tale into a PowerPoint presentation. Record the narration of your tale to go with your presentation.	35		
	Write your own fairy tale, and include a story map to help you brainstorm.	35		
	Pretend you are the villain in your fairy tale and rewrite it from your point of view.	40		
	Free choice: must be outlined on a proposal form and approved before beginning work.	10–40 points		
	Total number of points you are planning to earn from Side 1.	**Total points earned from Side 1:**		
	Total number of points you are planning to earn from Side 2.	**Total points earned from Side 2:**		
		Grand Total (/100)		

I am planning to complete _____ activities that could earn up to a total of _____ points.

Teacher's initials _____ Student's signature _____

Name: _____

Fairy Tales: Side 1

Guidelines:
1. You may complete as many of the activities listed within the time period.
2. You may choose any combination of activities.
3. Your goal is 100 points. You may earn up to _____ points extra credit.
4. You may be as creative as you like within the guidelines listed below.
5. You must show your plan to your teacher by _____.
6. Activities may be turned in at any time during the working time period. They will be graded and recorded on this sheet as you continue to work, so keep it safe!

Plan to Do	Activity to Complete (Side 1: 15–25 points)	Point Value	Date Completed	Points Earned
	Complete a story map for your fairy tale.	15		
	Complete another student's crossword puzzle.	15		
	Create a character mobile to show the characters in your fairy tale. Be sure to include information about each.	20		
	Choose an important character (other than the main character) in your fairy tale and make a puppet for that character.	20		
	Create a crossword puzzle with information from your fairy tale.	20		
	Create a three-dimensional timeline that shows all of the events in your fairy tale.	20		
	The main character has lots of adventures in your fairy tale. Make a scrapbook to show his or her experiences.	20		
	Create a diorama of your favorite scene from your fairy tale.	20		
	Draw a map to show all of the important places in your fairy tale.	25		
	Choose a job that one of the characters in your fairy tale does. Create an advertisement for the job.	25		
	Write three facts and a fib about the villain in your fairy tale.	25		
	Read two different versions of your fairy tale. Use a Venn diagram to compare and contrast them.	25		
	Total number of points you are planning to earn from Side 1.	**Total points earned from Side 1:**		

Name: _____ ●

Fairy Tales: Side 2

Guidelines:
1. You may complete as many of the activities listed within the time period.
2. You may choose any combination of activities.
3. Your goal is 100 points. You may earn up to _____ points extra credit.
4. You may be as creative as you like within the guidelines listed below.
5. You must show your plan to your teacher by _____.
6. Activities may be turned in at any time during the working time period. They will be graded and recorded on this sheet as you continue to work, so keep it safe!

Plan to Do	Activity to Complete (Side 2: 30–35 points)	Point Value	Date Completed	Points Earned
	Turn your fairy tale into a board game.	30		
	Prepare a news report that tells about the most important thing that happens in your fairy tale.	30		
	Most fairy tales have an object that plays an important role. Make a model of the object in your fairy tale. Label its important parts.	30		
	Pretend that you are the villain in your fairy tale and rewrite it from your point of view.	30		
	Write at least three diary entries for one character in your fairy tale.	30		
	Turn your fairy tale into a PowerPoint presentation. Record the narration of your tale to go with your presentation.	35		
	Write your own fairy tale, and include a story map to help you brainstorm.	35		
	Free choice: must be outlined on a proposal form and approved before beginning work.	10–40 points		
	Total number of points you are planning to earn from Side 1.	**Total points earned from Side 1:**		
	Total number of points you are planning to earn from Side 2.	**Total points earned from Side 2:**		
		Grand Total (/100)		

I am planning to complete _____ activities that could earn up to a total of _____ points.

Teacher's initials _____ Student's signature _____

© Prufrock Press Inc. • *Differentiating Instruction With Menus for the Inclusive Classroom: Language Arts* • *Grades 3–5*

Folk Tales

2-5-8 Menus

Background Information

All folk tales have similar elements. Folk tales usually include:

- wishes being granted,
- magical objects being used throughout the story,
- animals talking,
- the use of trickery,
- the number three, and
- a poor person becoming rich.

Folk tales usually follow a predictable pattern. The stories often start very quickly so children are drawn into the story with ease. The characters are simplistic, and as they progress through the tale, the plots often seem predictable. Most problems do get resolved with a happy ending. See the Appendix for a book list of popular folk tales.

Reading Objectives Covered Through These Menus and These Activities

- Students will read from a variety of genres for pleasure and to acquire information.
- Students will interpret figurative language and multiple-meaning words.
- Students will show comprehension by retelling or acting out events in the story.
- Students will compare one literary work with another.
- Students will recognize distinguishing features of folk tales.

Writing Objectives Covered Through These Menus and These Activities

- Students will write to inform, explain, describe, or narrate.
- Students will write to entertain.
- Students will use vivid language.

Materials Needed by Students for Completion

- Poster board or large white paper
- Paper bags (for puppets)
- Socks (for puppets)

- Materials for three-dimensional timelines
- Story map of teacher's choice
- Shoe boxes (for dioramas)

Special Notes on the Use of These Menus

The circle menu gives students the option of surveying their classmates. Depending on their experiences, they may already be familiar with asking the survey questions, tallying results, and creating a way to show data. If this is not the case, most students quickly understand when shown an example of a completed survey.

Time Frame

- 1–2 weeks—Students are given the menus as the unit is started, and the teacher discusses all of the product options on the menus. As the different options are discussed, students will choose products that add up to a total of at least 10 points. As the lessons progress through the week, the teacher and students refer back to the options associated with the content being taught.
- 1–2 days—The teacher chooses an activity from the menus to use with the entire class.

Suggested Forms

- All-purpose rubric
- Student presentation rubric

Folk Tales

Directions: Choose at least two activities from the menu below. The activities must total at least 10 points. Place a check mark next to each box to show which activities you will complete. All activities must be completed by:_____.

---

2 Points
❐ Complete a story map for your folk tale.
❐ Make a poster that shows the elements found in folk tales.

---

5 Points
❐ Make a three-dimensional timeline that shows the events in your folk tale.
❐ Design a diorama that shows the setting and characters in your folk tale.
❐ Make a Venn diagram that compares and contrasts folk tales to tall tales.
❐ Create a brochure for a folk tale your choice. Include information to explain why others may want to read the tale.

---

8 Points
❐ Turn one of your favorite folk tales into a play. Use puppets to tell the tale.
❐ Create your own folk tale. Include a story map and a rough draft of your ideas.

Name: _____

Folk Tales

Directions: Choose at least two activities from the menu below. The activities must total at least 10 points. Place a check mark next to each box to show which activities you will complete. All activities must be completed by: _____.

---

2 Points
- ☐ Complete a story map for your folk tale.
- ☐ Make a three-dimensional timeline that shows the events in your folk tale.

---

5 Points
- ☐ Design a survey to discover your classmates' favorite folk tales. Record your data and design a way to present them.
- ☐ Design a diorama that shows the setting and characters in your folk tale.
- ☐ Make a Venn diagram that compares and contrasts folk tales to tall tales.
- ☐ Create a book cover for a folk tale of your choice.

---

8 Points
- ☐ Turn one of your favorite folk tales into a play. Use puppets to tell the tale.
- ☐ Create your own folk tale. Include a story map and a rough draft of your ideas.

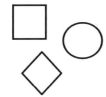
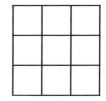

Alphabet Books

Three Shape Menu ▲ and Tic-Tac-Toe Menu ●

See the Appendix for a book list of popular alphabet books.

Reading Objectives Covered Through These Menus and These Activities
- Students will compare one literary work with another.
- Students will draw conclusions and make predictions on what is read in the story.

Writing Objectives Covered Through These Menus and These Activities
- Students will write to express their feelings, develop opinions, reflect, or problem solve.
- Students will write to inform, explain, describe, or narrate.
- Students will write to entertain.
- Students will exhibit voice in their writing.
- Students will use vivid language.

Materials Needed by Students for Completion
- Materials for board games (e.g., folders, colored cards)
- Paper bags (for puppets)
- Socks (for puppets)
- Microsoft PowerPoint or other slideshow software
- Index cards (for trading cards)
- Various alphabet books

Special Notes on the Use of These Menus
This topic has two different menu formats: Three Shape menu and Tic-Tac-Toe menu. The Three Shape menu is specifically selected for the triangle (lower level) option, as it easily allows the menu to be broken into manageable bits. The menu itself can be cut into strips of the same shape. Students can then be given a strip of square product choices for their use. Once they have chosen and submitted the square product for grading, they can be given the circle strip, and lastly, they can complete the diamond strip. Because this type of menu is designed to become more advanced as students move through the shapes, teachers may choose to

provide their students who have special needs with the top two shapes and save the diamonds for enrichment.

Time Frame
- 2 weeks—Students are given the menus as the unit is started. The teacher will go over all of the options for that content and have students note the activities they are most interested in completing. As the teacher presents lessons throughout the week, he or she should refer back to the options associated with that content. If students are using the Tic-Tac-Toe menu form, completed products should make a column or a row. If students are using the Three Shape menu form, they should complete one product from each different shape group. When students complete these patterns, they will have completed one activity from three different objectives, learning styles, or levels of Bloom's Revised taxonomy.
- 1 week—At the start of the unit, the teacher chooses the three activities he or she feels are most valuable for the students. Stations can be set up in the classroom. These three activities are available for student choice throughout the week, as regular instruction takes place.
- 1–2 days—The teacher chooses an activity from the menus to use with the entire class.

Suggested Forms
- All-purpose rubric
- Free-choice proposal form

Alphabet Books

Directions: Choose one activity from each shape group. Circle one choice from each group of shapes. Color in the shape after you have finished it. All activities must be completed by: _____.

Convert an alphabet book of your choice into a song or rap. Share your new song with your classmates.

Read one of Jerry Pallotta's alphabet books. Make a book cover for the book.

Make a set of trading cards for at least six alphabet books. Include reasons why people would enjoy each one.

After choosing an alphabet book, create a puppet unique to your chosen book that could be used to narrate that book.

Create an ABC-themed board game. Your question and activity cards should follow the theme.

Free choice—Submit a free-choice proposal form to your teacher for approval.

Create an alphabet book of books. Think of all of the books you have read and create an alphabet book with one page for each book.

Choose a topic from social studies. Create an acrostic for the topic. Use this to create your own alphabet book.

W rite the word
O val letters
R emember the word
D raw a picture

Think of a topic you enjoy in science. Create an alphabet PowerPoint that shares ideas for this topic.

Name: _____ ●

Alphabet Books

Directions: Check the boxes you plan to complete. They should form a tic-tac-toe across or down. All products are due by: _____.

☐ *Make a Book Cover*	☐ *Create a Song or Rap*	☐ *Create a Book*
Read one of Jerry Pallotta's alphabet books. Make a book cover for the book.	Convert an alphabet book of your choice into a song or rap. Share your new song with your classmates.	Create an alphabet book of books. Think of all of the books you have enjoyed and create an alphabet book with one page for each book. Choose your illustrations carefully!
☐ *Create a PowerPoint*	☐ *Free Choice*	☐ *Make a Puppet*
Think of a topic you enjoy in science. Create an alphabet PowerPoint that shares ideas for this topic.	(Fill out your proposal form before beginning the free choice!)	After choosing an alphabet book, create a puppet unique to your book that could be used to narrate that book.
☐ *Design a Board Game*	☐ *Create an Acrostic*	☐ *Create Trading Cards*
Create an ABC-themed board game. Your question and activity cards should follow the theme.	Choose a topic from social studies. Create an acrostic for the topic. Use this to create your own alphabet book.	Make a set of trading cards for at least 10 alphabet books. Include reasons why people would enjoy each one.

© Prufrock Press Inc. • *Differentiating Instruction With Menus for the Inclusive Classroom: Language Arts* • *Grades 3–5*

Science Fiction

2-5-8 Menus

Background Information

All science fiction stories have similar elements. Science fiction stories usually include:

- newly developed innovations, usually in technology or science; and
- settings in a futuristic or other world.

Reading Objectives Covered Through These Menus and These Activities

- Students will show comprehension by summarizing the story.
- Students will analyze characters, their relationships, and their importance in the story.
- Students will represent textual information by using story maps.
- Students will compare one literary genre with another.
- Students will recognize distinguishing features of science fiction.

Writing Objectives Covered Through These Menus and These Activities

- Students will support their responses with textual evidence.
- Students will write to express their feelings, develop opinions, reflect, or problem solve.
- Students will write to inform, explain, describe, or narrate.
- Students will write to entertain.
- Students will exhibit voice in their writing.

Materials Needed by Students for Completion

- Materials for board games (e.g., folders, colored cards)
- Microsoft PowerPoint or other slideshow software
- Rulers (for comic strips)
- Story map of teacher's choice
- Shoe boxes (for dioramas)

Time Frame

- 1–2 weeks—Students are given the menus as the unit is started, and the teacher discusses all of the product options on the menus. As the different options are discussed, students will choose products that add up to a total of 10 points. As the lessons progress through the

week, the teacher and students refer back to the options associated with the content being taught.
- 1–2 days—The teacher chooses an activity from the menus to use with the entire class.

Suggested Forms
- All-purpose rubric

Science Fiction

Directions: Choose at least two activities from the menu below. The activities must total at least 10 points. Place a check mark next to each box to show which activities you will complete. All activities must be completed by:_____.

---

2 Points

❏ Create a mind map that shows all of the important elements found in a science fiction story.

❏ Make an acrostic for the phrase "science fiction." Use a phrase to describe this genre for each letter.

---

5 Points

❏ Take your favorite science fiction story and make a board game with the same theme.

❏ Create a diorama that shows a scene from your science fiction story.

❏ Create a comic strip that shows your favorite science fiction character and his or her next adventure.

❏ Complete a story map about a science fiction story of your choice.

---

8 Points

❏ Develop a PowerPoint presentation that teaches your classmates how to write a science fiction story.

❏ Write your own science fiction story set in the future. Include a story map that shows your prewriting.

Name: _____

Science Fiction

Directions: Choose at least two activities from the menu below. The activities must total at least 10 points. Place a check mark next to each box to show which activities you will complete. All activities must be completed by:_____.

---

2 Points

❐ Create a mind map that shows all of the important elements found in a science fiction story.

❐ Make an acrostic for the phrase "science fiction." Use a phrase to describe this genre for each letter.

---

5 Points

❐ Take your favorite science fiction story and make a board game with the same theme.

❐ Create a diorama that shows a scene from your science fiction story.

❐ Make a Venn diagram to compare and contrast science fiction with another genre.

❐ Create a comic strip that shows your favorite science fiction character and his or her next adventure.

---

8 Points

❐ Develop a PowerPoint presentation that teaches your classmates how to write a science fiction story.

❐ Write your own science fiction story set in the future. Include a story map that shows your prewriting, as well as your rough draft.

Mysteries

Three Shape Menu ▲ and Tic-Tac-Toe Menu ●

Reading Objectives Covered Through These Menus and These Activities
- Students will show comprehension by retelling or acting out events in the story.
- Students will show comprehension by summarizing the story.
- Students will recognize story problems or plot.
- Students will represent textual information by using story maps.
- Students will recognize distinguishing features of mysteries.

Writing Objectives Covered Through These Menus and These Activities
- Students will write to inform, explain, describe, or narrate.
- Students will write to entertain.
- Students will exhibit voice in their writing.

Materials Needed by Students for Completion
- Materials for board games (e.g., folders, colored cards)
- Video camera (for news reports and commercials)
- Blank index cards (for recipe cards and trading cards)
- Magazines (for collages)
- Story map of teacher's choice

Special Notes on the Use of These Menus
This topic has two different menu formats: Three Shape menu and Tic-Tac-Toe menu. The Three Shape menu is specifically selected for the triangle (lower level) option, as it easily allows the menu to be broken into manageable bits. The menu itself can be cut into strips of the same shape. Students can then be given a strip of square product choices for their use. Once they have chosen and submitted the square product for grading, they can be given the circle strip, and lastly, they can complete the diamond strip. Because this type of menu is designed to become more advanced as students move through the shapes, teachers may choose to provide their students who have special needs with the top two shapes and save the diamonds for enrichment.

Time Frame

- 2 weeks—Students are given the menus as the unit is started. The teacher will go over all of the options for that content and have students note the activities they are most interested in completing. As the teacher presents lessons throughout the week, he or she should refer back to the options associated with that content. If students are using the Tic-Tac-Toe menu form, completed products should make a column or a row. If students are using the Three Shape menu form, they should complete one product from each different shape group. When students complete these patterns, they will have completed one activity from three different objectives, learning styles, or levels of Bloom's Revised taxonomy.
- 1 week—At the start of the unit, the teacher chooses the three activities he or she feels are most valuable for the students. Stations can be set up in the classroom. These three activities are available for student choice throughout the week, as regular instruction takes place.
- 1–2 days—The teacher chooses an activity from the menus to use with the entire class.

Suggested Forms

- All-purpose rubric
- Free-choice proposal form

Name: _____ ▲

Mysteries

Directions: Choose one activity from each shape group. Circle one choice from each group of shapes. Color in the shape after you have finished it. All activities must be completed by: _____.

Think about all of the elements that make a good mystery. Create a recipe card that shows the ingredients of a well-written mystery.

Design a collage that shows examples of elements that can be found in mysteries.

Create a Venn diagram that compares and contrasts mysteries to another genre of your choice.

Read a mystery of your choice. Create a new book cover for the book that you choose.

After you have read your mystery, complete the story map.

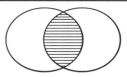 List at least five popular mysteries. Create a trading card for each book. Include the main characters and a description of the plot, but don't give away the ending!

Create a board game with a mystery-based theme. Be creative in your choice of pieces, game cards, and rules.

After reading a mystery, create a newspaper article that shares the mysterious events found in your story.

Maps often play an important role in mysteries. Create a map that might be used in a mystery.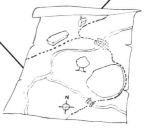

Name: _____

Mysteries

Directions: Check the boxes you plan to complete. They should form a tic-tac-toe across or down. All products are due by: _____.

☐ *Create a Board Game* Create a board game with a mystery-based theme. Be creative in your choice of pieces, game cards, and rules.	☐ *Prepare a Commercial* Prepare a commercial for your favorite mystery book that includes teasers to encourage people to read the book, but don't give away the ending!	☐ *Make a Venn Diagram* Create a Venn diagram that compares and contrasts mysteries to another genre of your choice.
☐ *Complete a Story Map* After you have read your mystery, complete the story map.	☐ **Free Choice** (Fill out your proposal form before beginning the free choice!)	☐ *Create a News Report* After reading a mystery, create a news report that shares the mysterious events found in your story.
☐ *Design a Book Cover* Read a mystery of your choice. Create a new book cover for the book that you choose.	☐ *Create a Recipe* Think about all of the elements that make a good mystery. Create a recipe card that shows the ingredients of a well-written mystery.	☐ *Create Trading Cards* Think of at least five popular mysteries. Create a trading card for each book. Include the main characters and a description of the plot, but don't give away the ending!

Plays

2-5-8 Menus

Reading Objectives Covered Through These Menus and These Activities

- Students will show comprehension by retelling or acting out events in the story.
- Students will show comprehension by summarizing the story.
- Students will represent textual information by using story maps.
- Students will compare different forms of a story (written vs. performed).

Writing Objectives Covered Through These Menus and These Activities

- Students will write to inform, explain, describe, or narrate.
- Students will write to entertain.
- Students will exhibit voice in their writing.
- Students will revise drafts.

Materials Needed by Students for Completion

- Poster board or large white paper
- Materials for three-dimensional timeline ▲
- Product cube template
- Story map of teacher's choice
- Paper bags (for puppets)
- Socks (for puppets)

Time Frame

- 1–2 weeks—Students are given the menus as the unit is started, and the teacher discusses all of the product options on the menus. As the different options are discussed, students will choose products that add up to a total of at least 10 points. As the lessons progress through the week, the teacher and students refer back to the options associated with the content being taught.
- 1–2 days—The teacher chooses an activity from the menus to use with the entire class.

Suggested Forms

- All-purpose rubric
- Student presentation rubric
- Point-based free-choice proposal form

Plays

Directions: Choose at least two activities from the menu below. The activities must total at least 10 points. Place a check mark next to each box to show which activities you will complete. All activities must be completed by:_____.

---

2 Points

☐ Read a play of your choice. Complete the story map of the play you read.

☐ Create a three-dimensional timeline that shows the events in your play.

---

5 Points

☐ Make your own puppet for a character in the play you are reading.

☐ Complete the plays cube.

☐ Read a play of your choice. Review the play in a newspaper article and include specific reasons why you liked or disliked the play.

☐ Free choice—Submit a free-choice proposal to your teacher for approval.

---

8 Points

☐ Choose one of your favorite fictional stories. Change this story into a play. Ask some of your class-mates to help you perform your play.

☐ Make a puppet show with at least two characters to share with your classmates.

☐ Stage directions are very important in a play. Select 1 minute of a sporting event and write the event as a play. Be sure to focus on the stage directions!

Plays

Directions: Choose at least two activities from the menu below. The activities must total at least 10 points. Place a check mark next to each box to show which activities you will complete. All activities must be completed by: _____.

---

2 Points

❏ Read a play of your choice. Complete a story map of the play you read.

❏ Complete the plays cube.

---

5 Points

❏ Make your own puppet for a character in the play you are reading.

❏ Stage directions are very important in a play. Select 1 minute of a sporting event and write the event as a play. Be sure to focus on the stage directions!

❏ Read a play of your choice. Review the play in a newspaper article and include specific reasons why you like or dislike the play.

❏ Choose one of your favorite fictional stories. Change this story into a play and submit the script to your teacher.

❏ Free choice—Submit a free-choice proposal form to your teacher for approval.

---

8 Points

❏ Write your own play to perform for your classmates. Ask some of your classmates to help you perform your play.

❏ Make a puppet show with at least two characters to share with your classmates.

Plays Cube

Complete the cube for the play you have read. Use this pattern or create your own cube. Respond to the items on each side to analyze your play in depth.

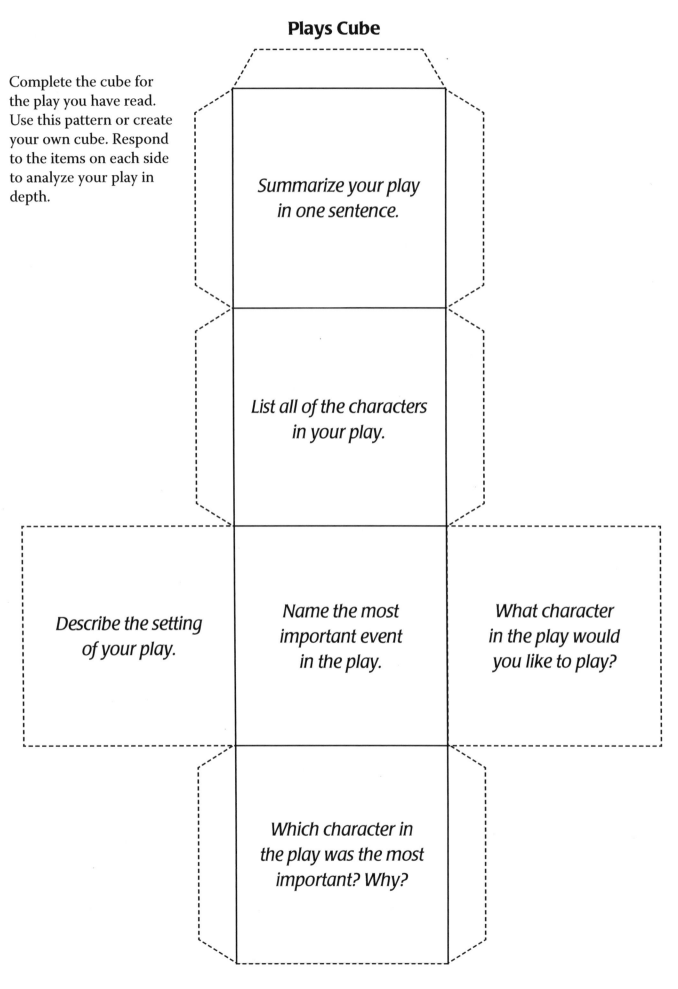

Summarize your play in one sentence.

List all of the characters in your play.

Describe the setting of your play.

Name the most important event in the play.

What character in the play would you like to play?

Which character in the play was the most important? Why?

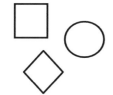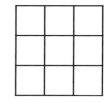

Poetry

Three Shape Menu ▲ and Tic-Tac-Toe Menu ●

Reading Objectives Covered Through These Menus and These Activities
- Students will recognize distinguishing features of cinquain, diamante, and haiku poems.

Writing Objectives Covered Through These Menus and These Activities
- Students will write to express their feelings.
- Students will write to inform, explain, describe, or narrate.
- Students will write to entertain.
- Students will exhibit voice in their writing.
- Students will use vivid language.

Materials Needed by Students for Completion
- Poster board or large white paper
- Magazines (for word collages)
- Shel Silverstein poetry books
- Product cube template
- Information sheet on different types of poems (p. 106)

Special Notes on the Use of These Menus

This topic has two different menu formats: Three Shape menu and Tic-Tac-Toe menu. The Three Shape menu is specifically selected for the triangle (lower level) option, as it easily allows the menu to be broken into manageable bits. The menu itself can be cut into strips of the same shape. Students can then be given a strip of square product choices for their use. Once they have chosen and submitted the square product for grading, they can be given the circle strip, and lastly, they can complete the diamond strip. Because this type of menu is designed to become more advanced as students move through the shapes, teachers may choose to provide their students who have special needs with the top two shapes and save the diamonds for enrichment.

Time Frame
- 2 weeks—Students are given the menus as the unit is started. The teacher will go over all of the options for that content and have stu-

dents note the activities they are most interested in completing. As the teacher presents lessons throughout the week, he or she should refer back to the options associated with that content. If students are using the Tic-Tac-Toe menu form, completed products should make a column or a row. If students are using the Three Shape menu form, they should complete one product from each different shape group. When students complete these patterns, they will have completed one activity from three different objectives, learning styles, or levels of Bloom's Revised taxonomy.

- 1 week—At the start of the unit, the teacher chooses the three activities he or she feels are most valuable for the students. Stations can be set up in the classroom. These three activities are available for student choice throughout the week, as regular instruction takes place.
- 1–2 days—The teacher chooses an activity from the menus to use with the entire class.

Suggested Forms

- All-purpose rubric
- Free-choice proposal form
- Student presentation rubric

Poetry

Directions: Choose one activity from each shape group. Circle one choice from each group of shapes. Color in the shape after you have finished it. All activities must be completed by: _____.

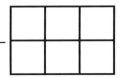

Create a windowpane of poetry with examples from at least three different poetry types (e.g., diamante, cinquain, haiku, free verse).

Create a poster that shows how to write diamante, cinquain, and haiku poems. Include an example of each on your poster.

Choose one type of poem and design a brochure that shares examples of this type of poem and what makes this type special.

Choose a poem from one of Shel Silverstein's poetry books. Create your own illustration for the poem you chose.

Choose one of your favorite poems and change it into a song or rap. Be prepared to share your creation with your classmates.

Using words from magazines, create a collage with at least 15 words that could be used if someone wrote a poem about you.

Write a poem about your classroom or classmates. Use either the diamante or the cinquain format.

Create a poetry cube with different phrases on each side that when rolled could create a poem.

Free choice poem—You choose the topic and the type!

Name: _____

Poetry

Directions: Check the boxes you plan to complete. They should form a tic-tac-toe across or down. All products are due by: _____.

☐ *Create a Cube* Create a poetry cube with different stanzas on each side that when rolled could create a poem.	☐ *Develop Your Own Song* Choose one of your favorite poems and change it into a song or rap. Be prepared to share your creation with your classmates.	☐ *Make a Windowpane* Create a windowpane of poetry with examples from at least three different poetry types (e.g., diamante, cinquain, haiku, free verse).
☐ *Design a Poster* Create a poster that shows how to write diamante, cinquain, and haiku poems. Include an example of each on your poster.	☐ **Free Choice** (Fill out your proposal form before beginning the free choice!)	☐ *Create a Collage* Using words from magazines, create a collage with at least 20 words that could be used if someone wrote a poem about you.
☐ *Illustrate a Poem* Choose a poem from one of Shel Silverstein's poetry books. Create your own illustration for the poem you chose.	☐ *Create a Questionnaire* Create a questionnaire that asks people whether they like poetry and which type of poem is their favorite. Present your findings on a poster.	☐ *Create a Poem* Write a poem about your classroom or classmates. Use either the diamante or the cinquain format.

 © Prufrock Press Inc. • *Differentiating Instruction With Menus for the Inclusive Classroom: Language Arts • Grades 3–5*

Poetry Cube

Complete a poetry cube. Each side of the cube should have a phrase or stanza on it. The cube should be designed so that when it is rolled three times, the three phrases it lands on can be used to write a poem. Use this pattern or create your own cube.

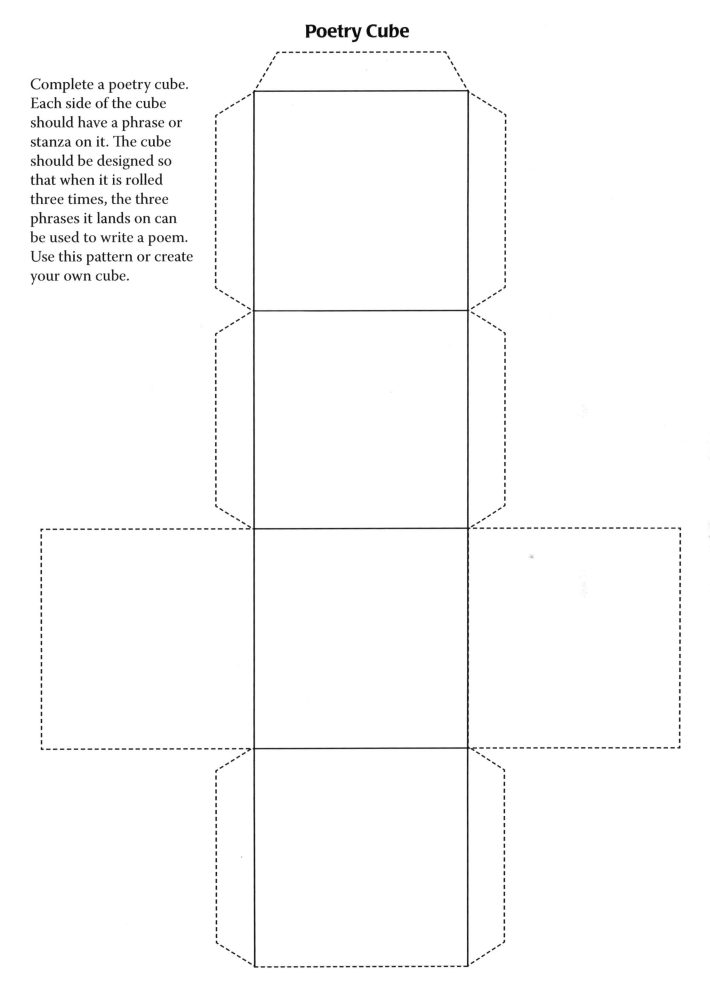

Types of Poems

Cinquain Poem

Line 1—a one-word title (usually two syllables)
Line 2—two words that describe your title (usually four syllables)
Line 3—three verbs or a three-word phase that describes an action relating to your title (usually six syllables)
Line 4—a four-word phrase that describes a feeling related to your title (usually eight syllables)
Line 5—one word that is another word for your title (usually two syllables)

Example:
Chadwick
Funny puppy
Running, jumping, barking
Chadwick—a magnificent dog
Scottie

Diamante Poem

Line 1—a one-word noun
Line 2—two adjectives that describe the noun in line 1
Line 3—three action verbs relating to noun in line 1
Line 4—four nouns that the words in line 1 and line 7 have in common
Line 5— three action verbs relating to the noun in line 7
Line 6—two adjectives that describe the noun in line 7
Line 7—one-word noun that is opposite of the noun in line 1

Example:
Sun
Warm, bright
Shines, heats, creates
Weather, beach, children, outdoors
Cools, waters, feeds
Fresh, welcome
Rain

Haiku Poem

Line 1—a five-syllable line
Line 2—a seven-syllable line
Line 3—a five-syllable line

Example:
Rain, it softly falls
Trees thirst and drink greedily
The forest sings out.

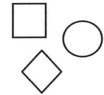
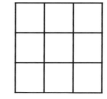

Nonfiction

Three Shape Menu ▲ and Tic-Tac-Toe Menu ●

Reading Objectives Covered Through These Menus and These Activities
- Students will show comprehension by summarizing the information in the book.
- Students will distinguish fact from opinion.

Writing Objectives Covered Through These Menus and These Activities
- Students will write to express their feelings, develop opinions, or reflect.
- Students will write to inform, explain, describe, or narrate.

Materials Needed by Students for Completion
- Materials for student-created models
- Magazines (for collages)
- Product cube template ▲
- Microsoft PowerPoint or other slideshow software
- Materials for board games
- Poster board or large white paper
- Coat hangers (for mobiles)
- Index cards (for mobiles)
- String (for mobiles)

Special Notes on the Use of These Menus
These menus allow students to select their own nonfiction topics that they would like to pursue. In order to facilitate these choices, some options instruct students to visit the library. In my experience, most librarians are more than happy to assist in book selection if they know ahead of time what the students need.

This topic has two different menu formats: Three Shape menu and Tic-Tac-Toe menu. The Three Shape menu is specifically selected for the triangle (lower level) option, as it easily allows the menu to be broken into manageable bits. The menu itself can be cut into strips of the same shape. Students can then be given a strip of square product choices for their use. Once they have chosen and submitted the square product for grading, they can be given the circle strip, and lastly, they can complete the diamond strip. Because this type of menu is designed to become more advanced as students move through the shapes, teachers may choose to provide their students who have special needs with the top two shapes and save the diamonds for enrichment.

Time Frame

- 2 weeks—Students are given the menus as the unit is started. The teacher will go over all of the options for that content and have students note the activities they are most interested in completing. As the teacher presents lessons throughout the week, he or she should refer back to the options associated with that content. If students are using the Tic-Tac-Toe menu form, completed products should make a column or a row. If students are using the Three Shape menu form, they should complete one product from each different shape group. When students complete these patterns, they will have completed one activity from three different objectives, learning styles, or levels of Bloom's Revised taxonomy.
- 1 week—At the start of the unit, the teacher chooses the three activities he or she feels are most valuable for the students. Stations can be set up in the classroom. These three activities are available for student choice throughout the week, as regular instruction takes place.
- 1–2 days—The teacher chooses an activity from the menus to use with the entire class.

Suggested Forms

- All-purpose rubric
- Free-choice proposal form
- Student presentation rubric

Name: _____ ▲

Nonfiction

Directions: Choose one activity from each shape group. Circle one choice from each group of shapes. Color in the shape after you have finished it. All activities must be completed by: _____.

Think of your favorite pastime or hobby. Create a poster that explains your hobby and why people might be interested in doing it.

Visit your library and find a book that discusses a hobby you enjoy. After reading the book, create a book cover that could be used for this book.

Choose your favorite hobby and visit the library to see what book it has on the topic. After looking at all of the books, make a mobile of the three books you think will be most interesting. Include why you think this.

Create a model that would help others understand your topic. Write a few paragraphs describing the details of your model.

After reading your nonfiction book, create a board game in which players learn about your topic.

Choose one topic in science or social studies that interests you. Read more information about the topic and prepare a PowerPoint presentation for your class on your findings.

Choose a book about a place you would like to visit. After reading the book, write a letter to your family describing your trip and the sights you saw.

Using magazines, create a collage that represents the topic you have read about. Write a paragraph to describe the collage and why you chose the pictures.

Create a fact cube on the topic you are reading about. On each side, include an important fact that you think your class-mates do not already know about the topic.

Name: _____

Nonfiction

Directions: Check the boxes you plan to complete. They should form a tic-tac-toe across or down. All products are due by: _____.

☐ *Prepare a PowerPoint*	☐ *Create a Mobile*	☐ *Create a Collage*
Choose one topic in science or social studies that interests you. After researching more information on the topic, prepare a PowerPoint presentation for your class on your findings.	Visit the library to see what books it has on your favorite hobby. After looking at all of the books, make a mobile of the four books you think will be most interesting. Include an explanation.	Using magazines, create a collage that represents the topic you have read about. Write a paragraph to describe the collage and why you chose the pictures you did.
☐ *Design a Model*	☐ **Free Choice**	☐ *Create a Brochure*
Create a model that would help others understand your topic. Write a few paragraphs describing the details of your model.	(Fill out your proposal form before beginning the free choice!)	Think of your favorite pastime or hobby. Create a brochure that explains your hobby, why people might be interested in doing it, and how they could get involved.
☐ *Create a Book Cover*	☐ *Write a Letter*	☐ *Create a Board Game*
Visit your library and find a book that discusses a hobby you enjoy. After reading the book, create a book cover that could be used for this book.	Choose a book about a place you would like to visit. After reading the book, write a letter to your family describing your trip and the sights you visited.	After reading your nonfiction book, create a board game in which players learn about your topic.

Nonfiction Cube

Complete a nonfiction cube. Each side of the cube should have an important fact that you think your classmates do not already know about your topic. Use this pattern or create your own cube.

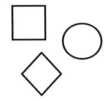

Biographies

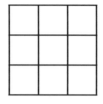

Three Shape Menu ▲ and Tic-Tac-Toe Menu ●

Reading Objectives Covered Through These Menus and These Activities
- Students will show comprehension by retelling or acting out events in a biography.
- Students will show comprehension by summarizing the events in the life of the subject of a biography.
- Students will analyze subjects, their relationships, and their importance in a biography.

Writing Objectives Covered Through These Menus and These Activities
- Students will write to inform, explain, describe, or narrate.
- Students will exhibit voice in their writing.
- Students will revise drafts.

Materials Needed by Students for Completion
- Microsoft PowerPoint or other slideshow software
- Materials for three-dimensional timelines
- Materials for trophies
- Empty cereal boxes
- Scrapbooking materials

Special Notes on the Use of These Menus
This topic has two different menu formats: Three Shape menu and Tic-Tac-Toe menu. The Three Shape menu is specifically selected for the triangle (lower level) option, as it easily allows the menu to be broken into manageable bits. The menu itself can be cut into strips of the same shape. Students can then be given a strip of square product choices for their use. Once they have chosen and submitted the square product for grading, they can be given the circle strip, and lastly, they can complete the diamond strip. Because this type of menu is designed to become more advanced as students move through the shapes, teachers may choose to provide their students who have special needs with the top two shapes and save the diamonds for enrichment.

Time Frame
- 2 weeks—Students are given the menus as the unit is started. The teacher will go over all of the options for that content and have students note the activities they are most interested in completing. As the teacher presents lessons throughout the week, he or she should refer back to the options associated with that content. If students are using the Tic-Tac-Toe menu form, completed products should make a column or a row. If students are using the Three Shape menu form, they should complete one product from each different shape group. When students complete these patterns, they will have completed one activity from three different objectives, learning styles, or levels of Bloom's Revised taxonomy.
- 1 week—At the start of the unit, the teacher chooses the three activities he or she feels are most valuable for the students. Stations can be set up in the classroom. These three activities are available for student choice throughout the week, as regular instruction takes place.
- 1–2 days—The teacher chooses an activity from the menus to use with the entire class.

Suggested Forms
- All-purpose rubric
- Free-choice proposal form
- Student presentation rubric

Name: _____ ▲

Biographies

Directions: Choose one activity from each shape group. Circle one choice from each group of shapes. Color in the shape after you have finished it. All activities must be completed by: _____.

Research an important person from history. Make a book cover that could be used for his or her autobiography.

Create a list of five people you view as being highly important. Choose one and read his or her biography. Create a PowerPoint presentation about his or her life and accomplishments.

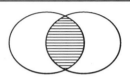

Create a Venn diagram to compare and contrast the person you read about to someone in your family.

Choose the four most important events in your person's life. Create a windowpane for the events and share why each was important.

Choose eight significant events in the life of the person in the biography. Using the dates for these events, create a three-dimensional timeline of the person's life.

After researching a famous person of your choice, think about the significant events in his or her life. Create a scrapbook about the person's life accomplishments.

Famous athletes are not the only people who can be featured on cereal boxes. After reading your person's biography, design a cereal box for him or her.

The person featured in your biography has been nominated for an award and will receive a trophy. Create a trophy that he or she might receive.

It is an honor to have a singer create a song especially for you. Either create your own song or select a song that you think represents the person you read about.

Name: _____

Biographies

Directions: Check the boxes you plan to complete. They should form a tic-tac-toe across or down. All products are due by: _____.

☐ *Make a Timeline* Choose 10 significant events in the life of the person in the biography. Using the dates of these events, create a three-dimensional timeline of the person's life.	☐ *Design a Cereal Box* Famous athletes are not the only people who can be featured on cereal boxes. After reading your person's biography, design a cereal box for him or her.	☐ *Create a Book Cover* Research an important person from history. Make a book cover that could be used for his or her autobiography.
☐ *Make a PowerPoint* Create a list of eight people you view as being highly important. Choose one and read his or her biography. Create a PowerPoint presentation about his or her life and accomplishments.	☐ **Free Choice** (Fill out your proposal form before beginning the free choice!)	☐ *Design a Trophy* The person featured in your biography has been nominated for an award and will receive a trophy. Decide which award your person might be receiving and create a trophy for him or her.
☐ *Sing a Song* It is an honor to have a singer create a song especially for you. Create a song especially written for your featured person. 	☐ *Make a Venn Diagram* Create a Venn diagram to compare and contrast the person you read about to someone you know. 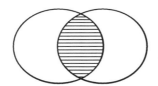	☐ *Create a Scrapbook* After researching a famous person of your choice, think about the significant events in his or her life. Create a scrapbook about the person's life accomplishments.

Genres

Game Show Menus

Reading Objectives Covered Through These Menus and These Activities
- Students will interpret figurative language and multiple-meaning words.
- Students will show comprehension by summarizing the story.
- Students will analyze characters, their relationships, and their importance in the story.
- Students will recognize distinguishing features of familiar genres.
- Students will compare different forms of a story (written vs. performed).

Writing Objectives Covered Through These Menus and These Activities
- Students will write to express their feelings, develop opinions, reflect, or problem solve.
- Students will write to inform, explain, describe, or narrate.
- Students will write to entertain.
- Students will exhibit voice in their writing.
- Students will use vivid language.

Materials Needed by Students for Completion
- Magazines (for collages)
- Poster board or large white paper
- Coat hangers (for mobiles)
- Index cards (for mobiles and trading cards)
- String (for mobiles)

Special Notes on the Use of These Menus
These menus ask students to create a postage stamp. There are not specific product guidelines for this product, as it is usually created on a poster, which has its own guidelines for evaluation. Of course, many students do not have much experience with traditional mail and thus do not always know what a postage stamp contains, so providing an image as an example is usually all they need to begin brainstorming.

Time Frame

- 2–3 weeks—Students are given the menus as the unit is started, and the guidelines and point expectations are discussed. As lessons are taught throughout the unit, the teacher and students can refer back to the options associated with that topic. The teacher will go over all of the options for the topic being covered and have students place check marks in the boxes next to the activities they are most interested in completing. As teaching continues during the next 2–3 weeks, activities are discussed, chosen, and submitted for grading.
- 1 week—At the start of the unit, the teacher chooses the three activities he or she feels are most valuable for the students. Stations can be set up in the classroom. These three activities are available for student choice throughout the week, as regular instruction takes place.
- 1–2 days—The teacher chooses an activity from the menus to use with the entire class.

Suggested Forms

- All-purpose rubric
- Point-based free-choice proposal form
- Student presentation rubric

Guidelines for Genres Game Show Menus

- You must choose at least one activity from each topic area.
- You may not do more than two activities in any one topic area for credit. (You are, of course, welcome to do more than two for your own investigation.)
- Grading will be ongoing, so turn in products as you complete them.
- All free-choice proposals must be turned in and approved prior to working on that free choice.
- You must earn **120** points for a 100%. You may earn extra credit up to _____ points.
- You must show your teacher your plan for completion by: _____.

Genres

Name: _____

Folk Tales	Tall Tales	Mystery	Poetry	Nonfiction	Biographies	Points for Each Level
☐ Make a mind map that shows the parts of your folk tale. (10 pts.)	☐ Create a mobile that shows the important parts of your favorite tall tale. (10 pts.)	☐ Create a set of trading cards for all of the characters in your mystery. (15 pts.)	☐ Write your favorite poem on a poster and illustrate it. (10 pts.)	☐ Create a collage of pictures related to a nonfiction topic of your choice. (10 pts.)	☐ Make a timeline showing 5–8 important events from the subject's life. (15 pts.)	10–15 points
☐ Play a role in a classmate's folk tale play. (20 pts.)	☐ Create a wanted poster for the main character in your tall tale. Be sure to focus on the character's personality! (25 pts.)	☐ Create a postage stamp for your favorite mystery. (25 pts.)	☐ Recite your favorite poem for the class. It should have at least six lines. (20 pts.)	☐ Create a must-know brochure about your topic. Include information that is important but is not usually known by others. (25 pts.)	☐ Write a journal entry about an important event in the life of the person you are reading about. (25 pts.)	20–25 points
☐ Pretend that you are one of the characters in your folk tale. Retell the folk tale from your point of view using expressive language. (30 pts.)	☐ Write a story about the next great adventure that would happen in your character's life. (30 pts.)	☐ Choose a topic in history or science and write your own mystery based upon this topic. (30 pts.)	☐ Write and illustrate your own haiku poem. (30 pts.)	☐ Write a song or rap about a nonfiction topic. It needs to include at least five details about the topic. (30 pts.)	☐ Come to class as the person in your biography. Share the top two ways you have impacted the world and made it a better place. (30 pts.)	30 points
Free Choice (prior approval) (25–50 pts.)	**Free Choice** (prior approval) (25–50 pts.)	**Free Choice** (prior approval) (25–50 pts.)	**Free Choice** (prior approval) (25–50 pts.)	**Free Choice** (prior approval) (25–50 pts.)	**Free Choice** (prior approval) (25–50 pts.)	25–50 points
Total:	**Total:**	**Total:**	**Total:**	**Total:**	**Total:**	**Total Grade:**

Name: _____

Genres

Folk Tales	Tall Tales	Mystery	Poetry	Nonfiction	Biographies	Points for Each Level
☐ Make a mind map that shows the parts of your folk tale. (10 pts.)	☐ Create a mobile that shows the important parts of your favorite tall tale. (10 pts.)	☐ Create a set of trading cards for all of the characters in your mystery. (10 pts.)	☐ Recite your favorite poem for the class. It should have at least six lines. (15 pts.)	☐ Create a collage of pictures related to a nonfiction topic of your choice. (10 pts.)	☐ Make a timeline showing 5–8 important events from the subject's life. (15 pts.)	10–15 points
☐ Pretend that you are one of the characters in your folk tale. Retell the folk tale from your point of view using expressive language. (25 pts.)	☐ Write a newspaper article documenting the adventures of a tall tale character. (25 pts.)	☐ Create a postage stamp for your favorite mystery. (20 pts.)	☐ Write and illustrate your own haiku poem. (25 pts.)	☐ Create a must-know brochure about your topic. Include information that is important but is not usually known by others. (20 pts.)	☐ Write a journal entry about an important life lesson you learned from reading about your individual. (25 pts.)	20–25 points
☐ Turn your folk tale into a play and perform it. (30 pts.)	☐ Write a story about the next great adventure that would happen in your character's life. (30 pts.)	☐ Choose a topic in history or science and write your own mystery based upon this topic. (30 pts.)	☐ Decide which type of poem is easiest to create. Write an example of this type of poem with a brief explanation about why you chose this type and why it is the easiest to create. (30 pts.)	☐ Write a song or rap about a nonfiction topic. It needs to include at least eight details about the topic. (30 pts.)	☐ Come to class as the person in your biography. Share the top two ways you have impacted the world and made it a better place. (30 pts.)	30 points
Free Choice (prior approval) (25–50 pts.)	**Free Choice** (prior approval) (25–50 pts.)	**Free Choice** (prior approval) (25–50 pts.)	**Free Choice** (prior approval) (25–50 pts.)	**Free Choice** (prior approval) (25–50 pts.)	**Free Choice** (prior approval) (25–50 pts.)	25–50 points
Total:	**Total:**	**Total:**	**Total:**	**Total:**	**Total:**	**Total Grade:**

CHAPTER 6

Writing

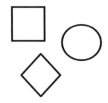
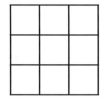

Parts of Speech

Three Shape Menu ▲ and Tic-Tac-Toe Menu ●

Reading Objectives Covered Through These Menus and These Activities
- Students will interpret figurative language and multiple-meaning words.

Writing Objectives Covered Through These Menus and These Activities
- Students will explain and use different parts of speech, including nouns, verbs, and adjectives.
- Students will write to express their feelings, develop opinions, reflect, or problem solve.
- Students will write to inform, explain, describe, influence, persuade, or narrate.
- Students will write to entertain.
- Students will exhibit voice in their writing.

Materials Needed by Students for Completion
- Poster board or large white paper
- Graph paper or Internet access (for crossword puzzles)
- Coat hangers (for mobiles)
- Index cards (for mobiles)
- String (for mobiles)
- Magazines (for collages)
- Scrapbooking materials
- Blank index cards (for concentration cards and trading cards)
- Product cube template

Special Notes on the Use of These Menus
This topic has two different menu formats: Three Shape menu and Tic-Tac-Toe menu. The Three Shape menu is specifically selected for the triangle (lower level) option, as it easily allows the menu to be broken into manageable bits. The menu itself can be cut into strips of the same shape. Students can then be given a strip of square product choices for their use. Once they have chosen and submitted the square product for grading, they can be given the circle strip, and lastly, they can complete the diamond strip. Because this type of menu is designed to become more

advanced as students move through the shapes, teachers may choose to provide their students who have special needs with the top two shapes and save the diamonds for enrichment.

Time Frame

- 2 weeks—Students are given the menus as the unit is started. The teacher will go over all of the options for that content and have students note the activities they are most interested in completing. As the teacher presents lessons throughout the week, he or she should refer back to the options associated with that content. If students are using the Tic-Tac-Toe menu form, completed products should make a column or a row. If students are using the Three Shape menu form, they should complete one product from each different shape group. When students complete these patterns, they will have completed one activity from three different objectives, learning styles, or levels of Bloom's Revised taxonomy.

- 1 week—At the start of the unit, the teacher chooses the three activities he or she feels are most valuable for the students. Stations can be set up in the classroom. These three activities are available for student choice throughout the week, as regular instruction takes place.

- 1–2 days—The teacher chooses an activity from the menus to use with the entire class.

Suggested Forms

- All-purpose rubric
- Free-choice proposal form
- Student presentation rubric

Parts of Speech

Directions: Choose one activity from each shape group. Circle one choice from each group of shapes. Color in the shape after you have finished it. All activities must be completed by: _____.

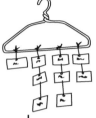

Make a mobile that shows examples of the different types of nouns.

Create a windowpane of your favorite 10 nouns. Include what types of nouns they are.

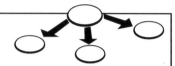

Create a mind map for the different types of nouns. Include at least five examples of each!

Create a collage of your favorite verbs using both words and pictures taken from magazines.

Create a cube with pictures and information about the verbs or activities you most enjoy.

Create a song or rap about verbs. Use examples from your daily life.

Create a "You're the Best!" poster for someone in your family. Include at least eight adjectives to describe what you like best about him or her.

Create a set of adjective trading cards. Choose at least five new adjectives that you might use in your writing this year.

Write and perform a play or skit about how the world would be different without adjectives.

Parts of Speech

Directions: Check the boxes you plan to complete. They should form a tic-tac-toe across or down. All products are due by: _____.

☐ *Nouns* Create a windowpane of your favorite 10 nouns. Include what types of nouns they are.	☐ *Adjectives* Write and perform a play or skit about how the world would be different without adjectives.	☐ *Verbs* Create a collage of your favorite verbs using both words and pictures taken from magazines.
☐ *Verbs* Create a cube with pictures and information about the verbs or activities you most enjoy.	☐ **Free Choice** (Fill out your proposal form before beginning the free choice!)	☐ *Adjectives* Create a set of adjective trading cards. Choose at least eight new adjectives that you might use in your writing this year.
☐ *Adjectives* Create a "You're the Best!" poster for someone in your family. Include at least 10 adjectives to describe what you like best about him or her.	☐ *Verbs* Make a scrapbook that is all about you, but focus on your favorite action verbs.	☐ *Nouns* Make a mobile that shows examples of the different types of nouns.

Parts of Speech Cube

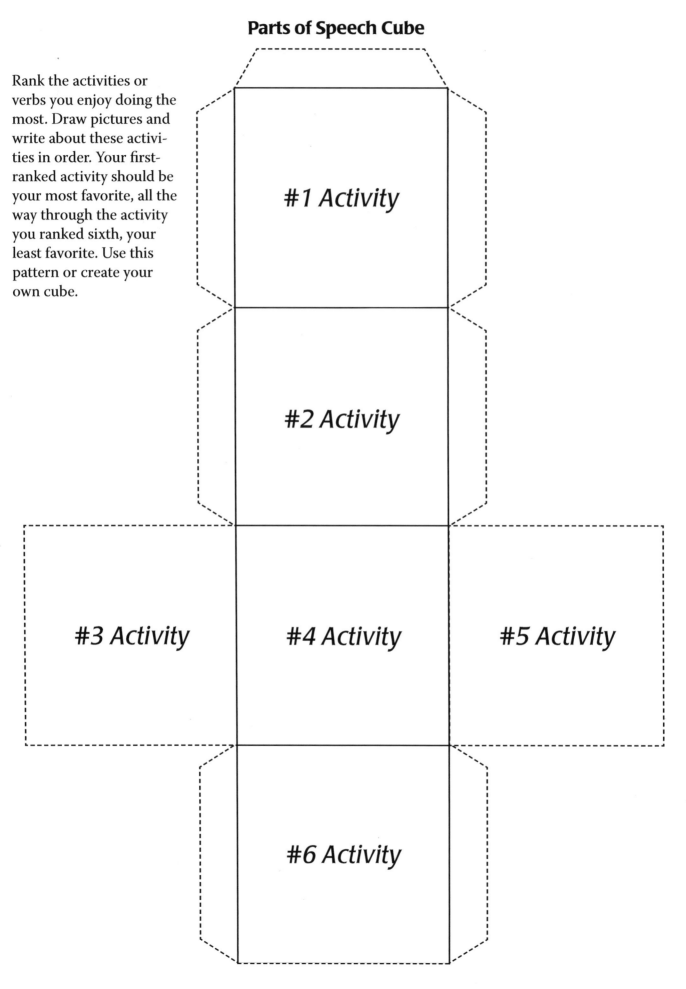

Rank the activities or verbs you enjoy doing the most. Draw pictures and write about these activities in order. Your first-ranked activity should be your most favorite, all the way through the activity you ranked sixth, your least favorite. Use this pattern or create your own cube.

#1 Activity

#2 Activity

#3 Activity

#4 Activity

#5 Activity

#6 Activity

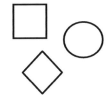

Spelling/Vocabulary I

Three Shape Menu ▲ and Tic-Tac-Toe Menu ●

Reading Objectives Covered Through These Menus and These Activities
- Students will use resources and references to build word meanings.
- Students will interpret figurative language and multiple-meaning words.

Writing Objectives Covered Through These Menus and These Activities
- Students will write to express their feelings, develop opinions, or reflect.
- Students will write to inform, explain, describe, or narrate.

Materials Needed by Students for Completion
- Graph paper or Internet access (for crossword puzzles)
- Blank index cards (for concentration cards)
- Product cube template

Special Notes on the Use of These Menus
These menus can be used for either spelling or vocabulary words, with a focus on the use of these words and their definitions. All activities will refer to the target words as "weekly words." The teacher will choose whether these are spelling or vocabulary words.

This topic has two different menu formats: Three Shape menu and Tic-Tac-Toe menu. The Three Shape menu is specifically selected for the triangle (lower level) option, as it easily allows the menu to be broken into manageable bits. The menu itself can be cut into strips of the same shape. Students can then be given a strip of square product choices for their use. Once they have chosen and submitted the square product for grading, they can be given the circle strip, and lastly, they can complete the diamond strip. Because this type of menu is designed to become more advanced as students move through the shapes, teachers may choose to provide their students who have special needs with the top two shapes and save the diamonds for enrichment.

Time Frame

- 1 week—For individual work, students are given the menus at the beginning of the week along with their weekly words. The teacher will go over all of the options for using the words and will have students note the activities they are most interested in completing. As the week continues, activities chosen and completed should make a column or a row if students are completing the Tic-Tac-Toe menu. If students are completing the Three Shape menu, then they should complete an activity from each shape group. Alternatively, these menus (or chosen activities from the menus) can be placed at centers, and students can choose which activities they would like to complete for the week. If the teacher uses one activity and a free-choice option each week, then an 8-week rotation could be used in a spelling center.
- 1–2 days—The teacher chooses an activity from the menus to use with the entire class.

Suggested Forms

- All-purpose rubric
- Free-choice proposal form

Spelling/Vocabulary I

Directions: Choose one activity from each shape group. Circle one choice from each group of shapes. Color in the shape after you have finished it. All activities must be completed by: _____.

Write the word
Oval letters
Remember the word
Draw a picture

Make an acrostic for two of your weekly words. The words you choose for each letter should be related to the words written downward.

Create a set of concentration cards for your weekly words. On one set of cards, use the word. The other set can have a picture or a written definition for each.

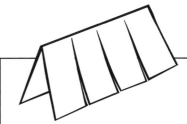

Create a flipbook for your weekly words with the word on the outside and a definition and a picture on the inside.

Choose four of your weekly words that you have trouble remembering. Develop some hand motions to help you remember them and share them with your classmates.

Using at least four of your weekly words, create a song or rap that could help your classmates learn the spelling and meaning of each one.

Complete a spelling cube for six of your weekly words.

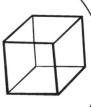

Write a letter to your parents or one of your classmates. Use at least half of your weekly words in your letter and make sure they are used correctly.

Using all of your weekly words, write a children's book about a wacky scientist.

Free choice— Submit a free-choice proposal form that explains what you would like to write using your weekly words.

Name: _____

Spelling/Vocabulary I

Directions: Check the boxes you plan to complete. They should form a tic-tac-toe across or down. All products are due by: _____.

☐ *Compose a Letter* Write a letter to your parents or one of your classmates. Use at least half of your weekly words in your letter, and make sure they are used correctly.	☐ *Concentrate* Create a set of concentration cards for your weekly words. On one set of cards, use the words. The other set can have corresponding pictures or written definitions.	☐ *Design Gestures* Choose four of your weekly words that you have trouble remembering. Develop some hand motions to help you remember them, and share your gestures with your classmates.
☐ *Create a Cube* Complete a spelling cube for six of your weekly words.	☐ **Free Choice** (Fill out your proposal form before beginning the free choice!)	☐ *Make an Acrostic* Make an acrostic for two of your weekly words. The words you choose for each letter should be related to the words written downwards. W rite the word O val letters R emember the word D raw a picture
☐ *Create a Crossword Puzzle* Using all of your weekly words, create a crossword puzzle. You can be creative on the clues that you use. Do not always use the definition for your clues!	☐ *Make a Spelling Song or Rap* Using at least half of your weekly words, create a song or rap that could help your classmates learn the spelling and meaning of each word.	☐ *Write a Children's Book* Using all of your weekly words, write a children's book about a wacky scientist.

Spelling Cube

Each side of this cube should have one of your weekly words, a definition for that word, and a picture that describes the word. Use this pattern or create your own cube.

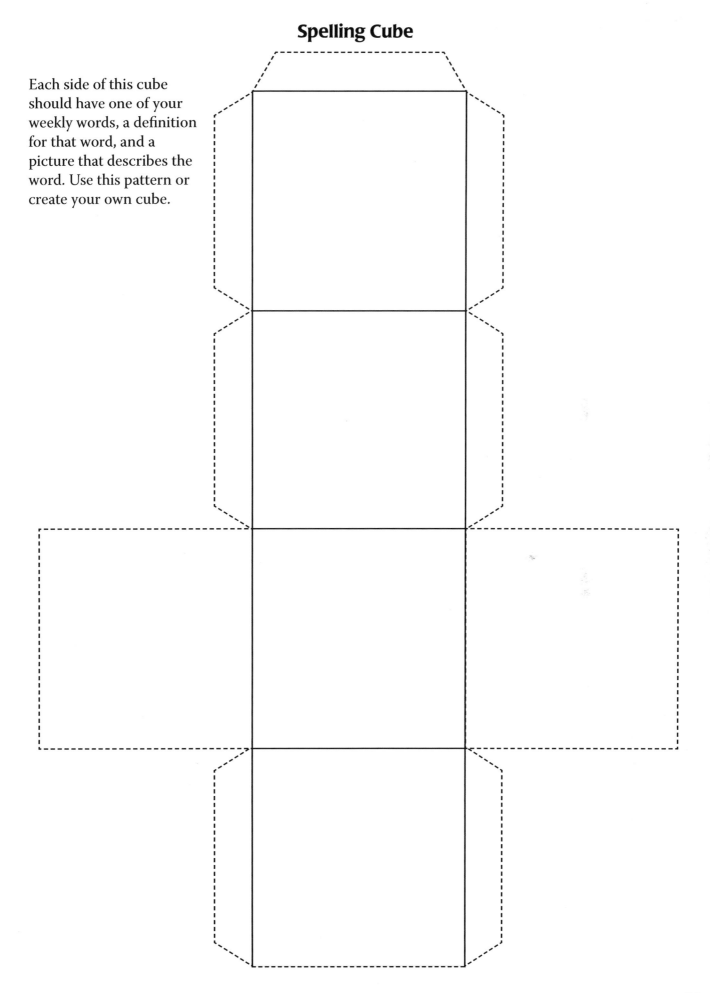

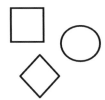

Spelling/Vocabulary II

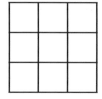

Three Shape Menu ▲ and Tic-Tac-Toe Menu ●

Reading Objectives Covered Through These Menus and These Activities
- Students will use resources and references to build word meanings.
- Students will interpret figurative language and multiple-meaning words.

Writing Objectives Covered Through These Menus and These Activities
- Students will write to inform, explain, describe, or narrate.

Materials Needed by Students for Completion
- Blank index cards (for trading cards and concentration cards)
- Materials for board games (e.g., folders, colored cards)
- Coat hangers (for mobiles)
- Index cards (for mobiles)
- String (for mobiles)
- Rulers (for comic strips)

Special Notes on the Use of These Menus
These menus can be used for either spelling or vocabulary words, with a focus on the dissection of the words and the use of prefixes and suffixes to build new words. All activities will refer to the target words as "weekly words." The teacher will choose whether these are spelling or vocabulary words.

This topic has two different menu formats: Three Shape menu and Tic-Tac-Toe menu. The Three Shape menu is specifically selected for the triangle (lower level) option, as it easily allows the menu to be broken into manageable bits. The menu itself can be cut into strips of the same shape. Students can then be given a strip of square product choices for their use. Once they have chosen and submitted the square product for grading, they can be given the circle strip, and lastly, they can complete the diamond strip. Because this type of menu is designed to become more advanced as students move through the shapes, teachers may choose to provide their students who have special needs with the top two shapes and save the diamonds for enrichment.

Time Frame

- 1 week—For individual work, students are given the menus at the beginning of the week with their weekly words. The teacher will go over all of the options for using the words and have students note the activities they are most interested in completing. As the week continues, activities chosen and completed should make a column or a row if students are competing the Tic-Tac-Toe menu; if students are completing the Three Shape menu, they should complete one activity from each shape group. Alternatively, these menus (or chosen activities from the menus) can be placed at centers, and students can choose which activities they would like to complete for the week. If the teacher uses one activity and a free-choice option each week, this could form an 8-week rotation for a spelling center.
- 1–2 days—The teacher chooses an activity from the menus to use with the entire class.

Suggested Forms

- All-purpose rubric
- Free-choice proposal form

Spelling/Vocabulary II

Directions: Choose one activity from each shape group. Circle one choice from each group of shapes. Color in the shape after you have finished it. All activities must be completed by: _____.

Using all of your words for this week, categorize them into nouns, verbs, adjectives, and pronouns.

Develop a set of trading cards with the definitions and pictures for your weekly words. Include on each card whether the word is a noun, verb, adjective, or pronoun.

Make a parts of speech mobile using all of your weekly words. Be creative in how you design the mobile to show the part of speech represented by each word.

Using your creativity, create a comic strip that uses at least four of your words for this week.

Choose two of your weekly words. Looking at all of the letters, record all of the shorter words that could be made with these letters.

Using the word calculator below, calculate the value of five of your weekly words.

Using all of your words for this week, identify new words by adding prefixes and suffixes. Record the new words you have created and their definitions.

Create a board game using your weekly words in which players get to practice the meanings of the new words created when prefixes are added to the weekly words.

Create a set of concentration cards in which players match each weekly word with a new word created by adding a prefix or suffix.

Word Calculator

A	B	C	D	E	F	G	H	I	J	K	L	M
4¢	5¢	2¢	3¢	4¢	6¢	9¢	1¢	7¢	10¢	8¢	2¢	5¢
N	O	P	Q	R	S	T	U	V	W	X	Y	Z
6¢	9¢	5¢	8¢	4¢	12¢	2¢	5¢	14¢	3¢	13¢	15¢	40¢

Spelling/Vocabulary II

Directions: Check the boxes you plan to complete. They should form a tic-tac-toe across or down. All products are due by: _____.

☐ *Create a Categorization Chart* Using all of your words for this week, categorize the words into nouns, verbs, adjectives, and pronouns.	☐ *Create a Comic Strip* Using your creativity, create a comic strip that uses at least four of your words for this week. 	☐ *Develop a Set of Trading Cards* Develop a set of trading cards for your weekly words. For each new word, share examples that could be created by adding prefixes and suffixes.
☐ *Make a Mobile* Make a parts of speech mobile using all of your weekly words. Be creative in how you design the mobile to show the part of speech represented by each word.	☐ **Free Choice** (Fill out your proposal form before beginning the free choice!)	☐ *Dissect a Word* Choose two of your weekly words. Looking at all of the letters, record all of the shorter words that could be made with those letters.
☐ *Calculate a Word's Value* Using the word calculator below, calculate the value of five of your weekly words.	☐ *Create a Board Game* Design a board game in which players are asked to decide if a new word can be created by adding prefixes and suffixes to your weekly words.	☐ *Identify New Words* Using all of your words for this week, identify new words by adding prefixes and suffixes. Record the new words you have created and their definitions.

Word Calculator

A	B	C	D	E	F	G	H	I	J	K	L	M
4¢	5¢	2¢	3¢	4¢	6¢	9¢	1¢	7¢	10¢	8¢	2¢	5¢
N	O	P	Q	R	S	T	U	V	W	X	Y	Z
6¢	9¢	5¢	8¢	4¢	12¢	2¢	5¢	14¢	3¢	13¢	15¢	40¢

Word Play

Game Show Menus

Reading Objectives Covered Through These Menus and These Activities
- Students will use resources and references to build word meanings.
- Students will interpret figurative language and multiple-meaning words.

Writing Objectives Covered Through These Menus and These Activities
- Students will write to inform, explain, describe, or narrate.
- Students will write to entertain.
- Students will exhibit voice in their writing.
- Students will use vivid language.

Materials Needed by Students for Completion
- Poster board or large white paper
- Materials for board games (e.g., folders, colored cards)
- Coat hangers (for mobiles)
- Index cards (for mobiles)
- String (for mobiles)
- Dictionaries and thesauri
- Graph paper or Internet access (for crossword puzzles)
- Microsoft PowerPoint or other slideshow software
- Blank index cards (for concentration cards)

Special Notes on the Use of These Menus
One of the activities for these menus has students design their own children's book based on antonyms. A wonderful example is *Is It Dark? Is It Light?* by Mary D. Lankford.

Time Frame
- 1–3 weeks—These menus can be taught as a separate unit, but they work best when used in conjunction with weekly words or a novel study. The menus can be given to students with the expectation that by the end of a grading period, a student will have completed 90 points in the four areas.

- 1–2 days—The teacher chooses an activity to use with the entire class during that lesson time or at a center.

Suggested Forms

- All-purpose rubric
- Point-based free-choice proposal form
- Student presentation rubric

Guidelines for Word Play Game Show Menus

- You must choose at least one activity from each topic area.
- You may not do more than two activities in any one topic area for credit. (You are, of course, welcome to do more than two for your own investigation.)
- Grading will be ongoing, so turn in products as you complete them.
- All free-choice proposals must be turned in and approved prior to working on that free choice.
- You must earn **90** points for a 100%. You may earn extra credit up to _____ points.
- You must show your teacher your plan for completion by: _____.

Name: _____

Word Play

	Homophones	Synonyms	Antonyms	Multiple-Meaning Words	Points for Each Level
	☐ Make a mobile with at least four sets of common homophones. (10 pts.)	☐ Make a set of concentration cards for at least 10 pairs of synonyms. (15 pts.)	☐ Make a windowpane of antonyms with at least eight sets of words. (10 pts.)	☐ Using a dictionary, look up the word "run." Make a poster showing pictures for at least half of the definitions for run. (15 pts.)	10–15 points
	☐ Complete the homophone brainstorming activity. (20 pts.)	☐ Create two word webs: one for the word "good," and one for the word "nice." Brainstorm synonyms for these words that could be used in your writing instead. (25 pts.)	☐ Create three facts and a fib about antonyms. (25 pts.)	☐ Design a crossword puzzle with at least four multiple-meaning words. (25pts.)	20–25 points
	☐ Design a board game for your classmates that tests their knowledge of homophones. (30 pts.)	☐ Write a funny yet descriptive story about a day in the life of a bug. Warning: You cannot use any of the words in the chart at the bottom of this page. (30 pts.)	☐ Design your own children's 20 questions book using antonyms to describe the final mystery object. (30 pts.)	☐ Perform a song or rap that includes at least five multiple-meaning words used more than once with different meanings. (30 pts.)	30 points
	Free Choice (prior approval) (25–50 pts.)	**Free Choice** (prior approval) (25–50 pts.)	**Free Choice** (prior approval) (25–50 pts.)	**Free Choice** (prior approval) (25–50 pts.)	25–50 points
	Total:	Total:	Total:	Total:	Total Grade:

Banned List of Words

good	bad	fun	like	said	hot
cold	happy	sad	mad	go	blue

Word Play

Homophones	Synonyms	Antonyms	Multiple-Meaning Words	Points for Each Level
☐ Complete the homophone brainstorming activity. (15 pts.)	☐ Make a set of concentration cards for at least 10 pairs of synonyms. (10 pts.)	☐ Make a windowpane of antonyms with at least 10 sets of words. (10 pts.)	☐ Using a dictionary, look up the word "run." Make a poster showing pictures for at least half of the definitions for run. (15 pts.)	10–15 points
☐ Design a board game for your classmates that tests their knowledge of homophones. (20 pts.)	☐ Create two word webs: one for the word "good," and one for the word "nice." Brainstorm synonyms for these words that could be used in your writing instead. (20 pts.)	☐ Create a funny greeting card for someone's birthday that uses only the antonyms of regularly used greeting card words. (25 pts.)	☐ Design a crossword puzzle with at least five multiple-meaning words. (20 pts.)	20–25 points
☐ Write a poem using at least 10 different sets of homophones. (30 pts.)	☐ Write a funny yet descriptive story about a day in the life of a bug. Warning: You cannot use any of the words in the chart at the bottom of this page. (30 pts.)	☐ Design your own children's 20 questions book using antonyms to describe the final mystery object. (30 pts.)	☐ Perform a song or rap that includes at least five multiple-meaning words used more than once with different meanings. (30 pts.)	30 points
Free Choice (prior approval) (25–50 pts.)	**Free Choice** (prior approval) (25–50 pts.)	**Free Choice** (prior approval) (25–50 pts.)	**Free Choice** (prior approval) (25–50 pts.)	25–50 points
Total:	Total:	Total:	Total:	Total Grade:

Banned List of Words

good	bad	fun	like	said	hot
cold	happy	sad	mad	go	blue

Brainstorming Homophones

As you know, homophones are words that sound the same but have different spellings and meanings.

The Basics

Listed below is one word in a homophone pair. Write the other word in the pair.

Ate		Male	
Beach		Pale	
Days		Rain	
Great		Road	
Here		Seen	
Leek		Waste	

The Challenge

Your challenge is to write three sentences using a pair of homophones from the table above in the same sentence.

Example: I **heard** the loud, thundering **herd** of elephants.
Write your own sentences below.

1. _____

   _____

2. _____

   _____

3. _____

   _____

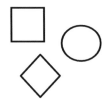

Reference Materials

Three Shape Menu ▲ and Tic-Tac-Toe Menu ●

Reading Objectives Covered Through These Menus and These Activities
- Students will use resources and references to build word meanings.

Writing Objectives Covered Through These Menus and These Activities
- Students will write to express their feelings, develop opinions, reflect, or problem solve.
- Students will write to inform, explain, describe, or narrate.
- Students will write to entertain.
- Students will exhibit voice in their writing.

Materials Needed by Students for Completion
- Poster board or large white paper
- Reference materials (dictionaries, thesauri, books with glossaries)
- Magazines
- Materials for board games (e.g., folders, colored cards)
- Coat hangers (for mobiles)
- Index cards (for mobiles)
- String (for mobiles)
- Blank index cards (for instruction cards)

Special Notes on the Use of These Menus
This topic has two different menu formats: Three Shape menu and Tic-Tac-Toe menu. The Three Shape menu is specifically selected for the triangle (lower level) option, as it easily allows the menu to be broken into manageable bits. The menu itself can be cut into strips of the same shape. Students can then be given a strip of square product choices for their use. Once they have chosen and submitted the square product for grading, they can be given the circle strip, and lastly, they can complete the diamond strip. Because this type of menu is designed to become more advanced as students move through the shapes, teachers may choose to provide their students who have special needs with the top two shapes and save the diamonds for enrichment.

Time Frame
- 2 weeks—Students are given the menus as the unit is started. The teacher will go over all of the options for that content and have students note the activities they are most interested in completing. As the teacher presents lessons throughout the week, he or she should refer back to the options associated with that content. If students are using the Tic-Tac-Toe menu form, completed products should make a column or a row. If students are using the Three Shape menu form, they should complete one product from each different shape group. When students complete these patterns, they will have completed one activity from three different objectives, learning styles, or levels of Bloom's Revised taxonomy.
- 1 week—At the start of the unit, the teacher chooses the three activities he or she feels are most valuable for the students. Stations can be set up in the classroom. These three activities are available for student choice throughout the week, as regular instruction takes place.
- 1–2 days—The teacher chooses an activity from the menus to use with the entire class.

Suggested Forms
- All-purpose rubric
- Free-choice proposal form

Reference Materials

Directions: Choose one activity from each shape group. Circle one choice from each group of shapes. Color in the shape after you have finished it. All activities must be completed by: _____.

Flipping from page to page in the dictionary is not the fastest way of finding words. Create a poster showing strategies and examples to find words quickly.

Create an instruction card for the proper use of a dictionary to find words.

There are many different kinds of dictionaries. Create a mind map that shows the different types and their uses.

Create a brochure or pamphlet that shows the structure of a glossary, as well as the benefits of using one.

Create a board game in which players need a glossary to answer questions and move through the game.

The glossaries of your textbooks have formed a complaint committee. They are unhappy that students do not use them. Create an advertisement to encourage students to use them.

Using the thesaurus, create a mobile with the words "great," "wonderful," and "big" as the top words. Provide at least five other words for each.

Choose an interesting picture from a magazine. Using a thesaurus, write a descriptive paragraph for the picture using all new words as descriptors.

Write a letter to a friend telling about the exciting uses for words found in a thesaurus. Be sure to include a few new words in your letter as examples.

Name: _____

Reference Materials

Directions: Check the boxes you plan to complete. They should form a tic-tac-toe across or down. All products are due by: _____.

☐ *Dictionary Skills* You can always find a word in the dictionary by flipping from page to page, but this is not the fastest way of finding words. Create a poster showing strategies and examples to find words quickly. 	☐ *Thesaurus Skills* The thesaurus is a great resource for expressive language. Using the thesaurus, create a mobile with the words "great," "wonderful," and "big" as the top words. Provide at least five other words for each.	☐ *Glossary Skills* The glossaries of your textbooks have gotten together and formed a complaint committee. They are very unhappy that students do not use them. Create an advertisement for their campaign to encourage students to use them.
☐ *Glossary Skills* Create a board game in which players need a glossary to answer questions and move through the game. 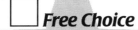	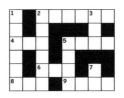 ☐ **Free Choice** (Fill out your proposal form before beginning the free choice!)	☐ *Thesaurus Skills* Write a letter to a friend telling about the exciting uses for words found in a thesaurus. Be sure to include a few new words in your letter as examples.
☐ *Thesaurus Skills* Choose an interesting picture from a magazine. Using a thesaurus, write a descriptive paragraph for the picture using all new words as descriptors.	☐ *Glossary Skills* Select a book that has a glossary. Create a crossword puzzle that would require using that glossary to solve. 	☐ *Dictionary Skills* Create an instruction card for the proper use of a dictionary to find words. Be creative! 

References

Anderson, L., & Krathwohl, D. (Eds.). (2001). *A taxonomy for learning, teaching, and assessing: A revision of Bloom's taxonomy of educational objectives* (Complete ed.). New York, NY: Longman.

Keen, D. (2001). *Talent in the new millennium: Report on year one of the programme.* Retrieved from http://www.dce. ac.nz/research/content _talent.htm

Magner, L. (2000). Reaching all children through differentiated assessment: The 2-5-8 plan. *Gifted Child Today, 23*(3), 48–50.

Mercer, C. D., & Lane, H. B. (1996). Empowering teachers and students with instructional choices in inclusive settings. *Remedial & Special Education, 17,* 226–236.

Appendix:
Book Lists

Fairy Tales

There are many books on fairy tales available; the books listed are just a few recommended by the author.

Andersen, H. C. (2004). *Thumbelina*. New York, NY: Dial Books.

Auch, M. J. (2005). *Chickerella*. New York, NY: Holiday House.

Aylesworth, J. (2003). *Goldilocks and the three bears*. New York, NY: Scholastic.

Beck, I. (1995). *Peter and the wolf*. New York, NY: Transworld.

Birdseye, T. (2001). *Look out, Jack! The giant is back!* New York, NY: Holiday House.

Braun, E. (2012). *Trust me, Jack's beanstalk stinks!: The story of Jack and the beanstalk as told by the giant*. Mankato, MN: Picture Window Books.

Calmenson, S. (1989). *The principal's new clothes*. New York, NY: Scholastic.

Climo, S. (1992). *The Egyptian Cinderella*. New York, NY: HarperCollins.

Climo, S. (1999). *The Persian Cinderella*. New York, NY: HarperCollins.

Coburn, J. R. (1998). *Angkat: The Cambodian Cinderella*. Auburn, CA: Shen's Books.

Cole, B. (2005). *Princess Smartypants rules*. New York, NY: Putnam.

Cooper, S. (2005). *The magician's boy*. New York, NY: Margaret K. McElderry Books.

Daly, N. (2007). *Pretty Salma: A Little Red Riding Hood story from Africa*. New York, NY: Clarion Books.

Daniels, P. (1980). *Sleeping beauty*. Milwaukee, WI: Raintree Children's Books.

Demarest, C. (2004). *Leaping beauty: And other animal fairy tales*. New York, NY: HarperCollins.

DePaola, T. (2002). *Adelita: A Mexican Cinderella story*. New York, NY: G. P. Putnam's Sons.

DePaola, T. (2006). *Little Grunt and the big egg: A prehistoric fairy tale*. New York, NY: Putnam.

Ensor, B. (2006). *Cinderella (as if you didn't already know the story)*. New York, NY: Schwartz & Wade Books.

French, V. (2000). *The Kingfisher book of fairy tales*. New York, NY: Kingfisher.

Galdone, P. (1985). *Rumpelstiltskin*. New York, NY: Clarion Books.

Hawkins, C. (2004). *Fairytale news*. Cambridge, MA: Candlewick Press.

Hooks, W. H. (1987). *Moss gown*. New York, NY: Clarion Books.

Hopkins, J. M. (2006). *The gold miner's daughter: A melodramatic fairy tale.* Atlanta, GA: Peachtree.

LaRochelle, D. (2007). *The end.* New York, NY: Arthur A. Levine Books.

Le Guin, U. (1992). *A rise on the red mare's back.* New York, NY: Orchard Books.

Lester, H. (2004). *Tackylocks and the three bears.* Westlake Village, CA: Sandpiper.

Levine, G. C. (2005). *Fairy dust and the quest for the egg.* New York, NY: Disney Press.

O'Malley, K. (2005). *Once upon a cool motorcycle dude.* New York, NY: Walker.

Pinkney, J. (1999). *The ugly duckling.* New York, NY: Morrow Junior Books.

Pullman, P. (2005). *Aladdin and the enchanted lamp.* New York, NY: Arthur A. Levine Books.

Squires, J. (2006). *The gingerbread cowboy.* New York, NY: HarperCollins.

Stanley, D. (2003). *Goldie and the three bears.* New York, NY: HarperCollins.

Stevens, J. (1987). *The three billy-goats Gruff.* San Diego, CA: Harcourt Brace.

Tolstoy, A. (1999). *The gigantic turnip.* Cambridge, MA: Barefoot Books.

Zunshine, T. (2004). *A little story about a big turnip.* New York, NY: Pumpkin House.

Folk Tales

There are many books on folk tales available; the books listed are just a few recommended by the author.

Ambrus, V. (1992). *Never laugh at bears: A Transylvanian folk tale*. New York, NY: Bedrick/Blackie.

Benitez, M. (1989). *How Spider tricked Snake*. Milwaukee, WI: Raintree.

Carter, A. (1989). *The twelve dancing princesses*. New York, NY: J. B. Lippincott.

Cauley, L. (1988). *The pancake boy: An old Norwegian folk tale*. New York, NY: Putnam.

Daise, R. (1997). *Little muddy waters: A Gullah folk tale*. Beaufort, SC: G.O.G. Enterprises.

Denman, C. (1988). *The little peacock's gift: A Chinese folk tale*. London, England: Blackie.

DePaola, T. (2007). *Tomie DePaola's front porch tales & north country whoppers*. New York, NY: G. P. Putnam's Sons.

Duff, M. (1978). *Rum pum pum: A folk tale from India*. New York, NY: Macmillan.

Hamilton, V. (1995). *Her stories: African American folktales, fairy tales, and true tales*. New York, NY: Blue Sky Press.

Hort, L. (1990). *The fool and the fish: A tale from Russia*. New York, NY: Dial Books.

Hunt, A. (1989). *Tale of three trees: A traditional folk tale*. Elgin, IL: Lion Publishing.

Jensen, N. (2000). *How flamingos came to have red legs: A South American folktale*. Bothell, WA: Wright Group.

Johnson-Davies, D. (2005). *Goha the wise fool*. New York, NY: Philomel Books.

Lodge, B. (1993). *Prince Ivan and the firebird: A Russian folk tale*. Boston, MA: Whispering Coyote.

Loverseed, A. (1990). *Tikkatoo's journey: An Eskimo folk tale*. London, England: Blackie.

Motomora, M. (1989). *Lazy Jack and the silent princess*. Milwaukee, WI: Raintree.

Muth, J. J. (2003). *Stone soup*. New York, NY: Scholastic.

Park, J. (2002). *The tiger and the dried persimmon: A Korean folk tale*. Toronto, ON, Canada: Douglas & McIntyre.

Scholey, A. (1989). *Baboushka: A traditional Russian folk tale*. Oxford, England: Lion.

Zemach, M. (1990). *It could always be worse: A Yiddish folk tale*. New York, NY: Farrar, Straus and Giroux.

Tall Tales

There are many books on tall tales available; the books listed are just a few recommended by the author.

Balcziak, B. (2003). *John Henry*. Minneapolis, MN: Compass Point Books.

Brimner, L. D. (2004). *Calamity Jane*. Minneapolis, MN: Compass Point Books.

Brimner, L. D. (2004). *Casey Jones*. Minneapolis, MN: Compass Point Books.

Brimner, L. D. (2004). *Davy Crockett*. Minneapolis, MN: Compass Point Books.

Dewey, A. (1987). *Gib Morgan, oilman*. New York, NY: Greenwillow Books.

Enderle, D. (2004). *The cotton candy catastrophe at the Texas state fair*. Gretna, LA: Pelican.

Gleiter, J. (1984). *Paul Bunyan and Babe the blue ox*. Milwaukee, WI: Raintree.

Gregg, A. (2000). *Paul Bunyan and the winter of the blue snow: A tall tale*. Spring Lake, MI: River Road.

Griffin, K. (2004). *The foot-stomping adventures of Clementine Sweet*. New York, NY: Clarion Books.

Hopkinson, D. (2008). *Abe Lincoln crosses a creek: A tall, thin tale (introducing his forgotten frontier friend)*. New York, NY: Schwartz & Wade Books.

Hopkinson, D. (2008). *Apples to Oregon: Being the (slightly) true narrative of how a brave pioneer father brought apples, peaches, pears, plums, grapes, and cherries (and children) across the plains*. New York, NY: Aladdin.

Hopkinson, D. (2009). *Stagecoach Sal: Inspired by a true tale*. New York, NY: Disney Hyperion Books.

Isaacs, A. (2000). *Swamp angel*. New York, NY: Puffin Books.

Jensen, P. (1994). *John Henry and his mighty hammer*. Mahwah, NJ: Troll Associates.

Jensen, P. (1994). *Johnny Appleseed goes a'planting*. Mahwah, NJ: Troll Associates.

Jensen, P. (1994). *Paul Bunyan and his blue ox*. Mahwah, NJ: Troll Associates.

Johnson, P. (1999). *Old Dry Frye: A deliciously funny tall tale*. New York, NY: Scholastic.

Kellogg, S. (1988). *Johnny Appleseed: A tall tale.* New York, NY: Mulberry Books.

Kellogg, S. (1992). *Mike Fink: A tall tale.* New York, NY: Mulberry Books.

Kellogg, S. (1992). *Pecos Bill: A tall tale.* New York, NY: Mulberry Books.

Kellogg, S. (1993). *Paul Bunyan: A tall tale.* New York, NY: Mulberry Books.

Kellogg, S. (1995). *Sally Ann Thunder and Whirlwind Crockett: A tall tale.* New York, NY: Mulberry Books.

Ketteman, H. (1998). *Heat wave!* New York, NY: Walker.

Kimmel, E. (2007). *The great Texas hamster drive.* New York, NY: Marshall Cavendish Children.

Lester, J. (1994). *John Henry.* New York, NY: Dial.

McKissack, P. (1991). *A million fish—more or less.* New York, NY: Random House.

Osborne, M. (1991). *American tall tales.* New York, NY: Scholastic.

Rossi, J. (1995). *The gullywasher.* Flagstaff, AZ: Northland.

Schur, M. (2009). *Gullible Gus.* New York, NY: Clarion Books.

Schwartz, A. (1975). *Whoppers: Tall tales and other lies.* (1975). Philadelphia, PA: Lippincott.

Shepard, A. (2001). *Master man: A tall tale of Nigeria.* New York, NY: HarperCollins.

White, L. (2002). *Comes a wind.* New York, NY: DK Ink.

Wood, A. (1996). *The Bunyans.* New York, NY: Blue Sky Press.

Alphabet Books

There are many alphabet books available; the books listed are just a few recommended by the author.

Berge, A. (2004). *Russia ABCs: A book about the people and places of Russia.* Minneapolis, MN: Window Picture Books.

Bonder, D. (2007). *Dogabet.* North Vancouver, BC, Canada: Walrus Books.

Bruchac, J. (2004). *Many nations: An alphabet of Native America.* New York, NY: Scholastic.

Cassie, B. (1995). *The butterfly alphabet book.* Watertown, MA: Charlesbridge.

Crane, C. (2001). *L is for lone star: A Texas alphabet.* Chelsea, MI: Sleeping Bear Press.

Cronin, D. (2005). *Click, clack, quackity-quack: An alphabetical adventure.* New York, NY: Atheneum Books for Young Readers.

Dahl, M. (2004). *Alphabet soup: A book of riddles about letters.* Minneapolis, MN: Picture Window Books.

Dahl, M. (2005). *Pets ABC: An alphabet book.* Mankato, MN: Capstone Press.

Fain, K. (1993). *Handsigns: A sign language alphabet.* San Francisco, CA: Chronicle Books.

Feelings, M. (1974). *Jambo means hello: Swahili alphabet book.* New York, NY: Dial.

Fisher, L. (1985). *Alphabet art: Thirteen ABCs from around the world.* New York, NY: Four Winds Press.

Haugen, B. (2004). *Canada ABCs: A book about the people and places of Canada.* Minneapolis, MN: Picture Window Books.

Heiman, S. (2003). *Australia ABCs: A book about the people and places of Australia.* Minneapolis, MN: Picture Window Books.

Heiman, S. (2003). *Germany ABCs: A book about the people and places of Germany.* Minneapolis, MN: Picture Window Books.

Hoberman, M. (1974). *Nuts to you & nuts to me: An alphabet of poems.* New York, NY: Knopf.

Joyce, S. (1998). *Alphabet riddles.* Columbus, NC: Peel Productions.

Leuck, L. (2003). *Jeepers creepers: A monstrous ABC.* San Francisco, CA: Chronicle Books.

MacDonald, R. (2003). *Achoo! Bang! Crash!: The noisy alphabet.* Brookfield, CT: Roaring Brook Press.

McLeod, B. (2006). *SuperHero ABC.* New York, NY: HarperCollins.

Murphy, M. (2002). *The alphabet keeper.* New York, NY: Alfred A. Knopf.

Pallotta, J. (1986). *The ocean alphabet book.* Watertown, MA: Charlesbridge.

Pallotta, J. (1989). *The yucky reptile alphabet book.* Watertown, MA: Charlesbridge.

Pallotta, J. (1990). *The jet alphabet book.* Watertown, MA: Charlesbridge.

Pallotta, J. (1991). *The dinosaur alphabet book.* Watertown, MA: Charlesbridge.

Pallotta, J. (1991). *The underwater alphabet book.* Watertown, MA: Charlesbridge.

Pallotta, J. (1994). *The spice alphabet book: Herbs, spices, and other natural flavors.* Watertown, MA: Charlesbridge.

Pallotta, J. (2002). *The skull alphabet book.* Watertown, MA: Charlesbridge.

Pallotta, J. (2004). *The beetle alphabet book.* Watertown, MA: Charlesbridge.

Rash, A. (2004). *Agent A to Agent Z.* New York, NY: Arthur A. Levine Books.

Schnur, S. (1999). *Spring: An alphabet acrostic.* New York, New York: Clarion Books.

Schroeder, H. (2004). *China ABCs: A book about the people and places of China.* Minneapolis, MN: Picture Window Books.

Schroeder, H. (2004). *Israel ABCs: A book about the people and places of Israel.* Minneapolis, MN: Picture Window Books.

Schroeder, H. (2004). *New Zealand ABCs: A book about the people and places of New Zealand.* Minneapolis, MN: Picture Window Books.

Schroeder, H. (2004). *The United States ABCs: A book about the people and places of the United States of America.* Minneapolis, MN: Picture Window Books.

Schwartz, D. (1998). *G is for googol: A math alphabet book.* Berkeley, CA: Tricycle Press.

Sobel, J. (2006). *Shiver me letters: A pirate ABC.* Orlando, FL: Harcourt.

Tapahonso, L. (1995). *Navajo ABC: A Diné alphabet book.* New York, NY: Macmillan Books for Young Readers.

Van Allsburg, C. (1987). *The alphabet theatre proudly presents the Z was zapped: A play in twenty-six acts.* Boston, MA: Houghton Mifflin.

Wargin, K. (2004). *M is for melody: A music alphabet.* Chelsea, MI: Sleeping Bear Press.

Wood, A. (2003). *Alphabet mystery.* New York, NY: Blue Sky Press.

Yorinks, A. (1999). *The alphabet atlas.* Delray Beach, FL: Winslow Press.

About the Author

After teaching science for more than 15 years, both overseas and in the U.S., **Laurie E. Westphal** now works as an independent gifted education and science consultant nationwide. She enjoys developing and presenting staff development on differentiation for various districts and conferences, working with teachers to assist them in planning and developing lessons to meet the needs of all students. Laurie currently resides in Houston, TX, and has made it her goal to convert as many teachers as she can to the differentiated lifestyle in the classroom and share her vision for real-world, product-based lessons that help all students become critical thinkers and effective problem solvers.

If you are interested in having Laurie speak at your next staff development day or conference, please visit her website, http://www.giftedconsultant.com, for additional information.

Common Core State Standards Alignment

This book aligns with an extensive number of the Common Core State Standards for ELA-Literacy. Please visit http://www.prufrock.com/ccss to download a complete packet of the standards that align with each individual menu in this book.

Additional Titles by the Author

Laurie E. Westphal has written many books on using differentiation strategies in the classroom, providing teachers of grades K–12 with creative, engaging, ready-to-use resources. Among them are:

 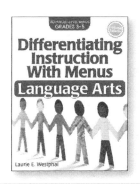  

Math, Language Arts, Science, and Social Studies volumes available for:

Differentiating Instruction With Menus, Grades K–2

Differentiating Instruction With Menus, Grades 3–5, Second Edition

Differentiating Instruction With Menus, Grades 6–8, Second Edition

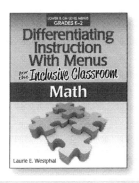 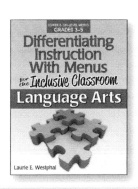  

Math, Language Arts, Science, and Social Studies volumes available for:

Differentiating Instruction With Menus for the Inclusive Classroom, Grades K–2

Differentiating Instruction With Menus for the Inclusive Classroom, Grades 3–5

Differentiating Instruction With Menus for the Inclusive Classroom, Grades 6–8

Literature for Every Learner, Grades 3–5; 6–8; and 9–12

Differentiating Instruction With Menus: Algebra I/II, Grades 9–12

Differentiating Instruction With Menus: Biology, Grades 9–12

For a current listing of Laurie's books, please visit Prufrock Press at http://www.prufrock.com.